Finding Meaning in Later Life

Finding Meaning in Later Life: Gathering and Harvesting the Fruits of Women's Experience is an exploration in understanding the psychological tasks inherent for women in creating and maintaining purpose as they mature and enter their later years. With ever-increasing lifespan for elders, it becomes important for a society that glorifies youth to meet the challenges of this developmental milestone.

Many books and articles on post-midlife are written from a biological and behavioral stance—with quantitative data supporting concrete lifestyle recommendations for "successful aging." Using this lens, successful aging is often defined as having good to excellent health, no disabilities in activities of daily living, good cognitive functioning, and living in the community. That "received wisdom" leads to the conundrum that the only path to successful aging is by not aging! This book challenges current thoughts on aging, expanding our perspective such that purpose and meaning in later years derives from inner resources that are not dependent on biological and physical states of being. Its conclusions stem from the direct experience and voices of mature women, obtained through qualitative research. The results of this study shed light on existential theories, bringing them to life with added weight and traction. Ultimately, the ideas explored here unfold as a map to navigate this often-misunderstood stage in life.

Marcia Nimmer received her Psy.D. from Pacifica Graduate Institute and was previously a licensed clinical social worker. She is currently working as a psychotherapist at the Wright Institute in Los Angeles. As a woman in her late fifties who began doctoral studies after raising five children, she became interested in the developmental stage that lies between midlife and old age. Her qualitative research on the subject of finding meaning in later life emerged as an outgrowth of her own personal journey.

Figure 1 The Harvest, 1882, by Camille Pissarro.

Finding Meaning in Later Life

Gathering and Harvesting the Fruits of Women's Experience

Marcia Nimmer

NEW YORK AND LONDON

First published 2018
by Routledge
711 Third Avenue, New York, NY 10017

and by Routledge
2 Park Square, Milton Park, Abingdon, Oxon, OX14 4RN

Routledge is an imprint of the Taylor & Francis Group, an informa business

© 2018 Taylor & Francis

The right of Marcia Nimmer to be identified as author of this work
has been asserted by her in accordance with sections 77 and 78 of
the Copyright, Designs and Patents Act 1988.

All rights reserved. No part of this book may be reprinted or
reproduced or utilized in any form or by any electronic,
mechanical, or other means, now known or hereafter invented,
including photocopying and recording, or in any information
storage or retrieval system, without permission in writing from the
publishers.

Trademark notice: Product or corporate names may be trademarks
or registered trademarks, and are used only for identification and
explanation without intent to infringe.

Library of Congress Cataloging-in-Publication Data
A catalog record for this title has been requested

ISBN: 978-0-8153-8294-2 (hbk)
ISBN: 978-1-351-13777-5 (ebk)

Typeset in Times New Roman
by Wearset Ltd, Boldon, Tyne and Wear

Contents

Acknowledgments	vi
1 The Need for a New Outlook	1
2 How We Age: Theories and Research	14
3 Women's Voices and Lived Experience: Existential Pursuits and Affirmation of Life	31
4 Women's Voices and Lived Experience: Human Relationships and Resiliency	48
5 Treatment Implications for Therapists Working with Older Adults	63
6 Where Do We Go from Here?	66
7 Final Thoughts: Big Data, Depth Psychology, and Poetry	73
Appendix A: Methodology	79
Appendix B: Screening and Interview Guides	87
References	88
Index	96

Acknowledgments

As I reflect on the creation of this book, I am profoundly aware that I have reached completion of this endeavor only as a result of support from family, friends, mentors, colleagues, and generously disposed participants who collectively carried me through this project. My own experience that growth and development throughout the lifespan is made possible by human connection nicely illustrates one of the main themes of this book, in a wonderful example of life imitating art. Friends from all walks of life supported me and lent help and guidance in making this research come to fruition. Further, the book's theory that generations need to cross boundaries and work together in order to benefit everyone played a synchronistic element in the publication of this book too. Talia Graff, the three-year-old girl I carpooled to nursery school in 1991, is the woman who brought this book idea to the attention of the publishing house in 2017. Who could have predicted that my nursery school charge would grow up and make me an author? I additionally want to thank all the editors at Routledge who made this dream a reality.

To my dear husband David, it is difficult to say enough. At a time in life in which he envisioned us having fewer commitments and more freedom, I took on doctoral studies and research that led to this book. He supported me through it all by accepting the demands put on my time, editing umpteen versions of first my dissertation and then this book, and immersing himself personally in the psychology world. This rite of passage belongs to him as much as it belongs to me.

To my participants, I will be eternally grateful to you for opening your hearts and lives, and illustrating what it means to make meaning in the second half of life. You have all touched me personally with your stories and reflections, joys and tribulations. My gratitude also extends to Mel Gottlieb, Ph.D. and Gilda Frantz, M.A. who were readers for this project. I especially want to thank Oksana Yakushko, Ph.D. who mentored me and is the silent author of the product you hold in your hands.

Acknowledgments   vii

The publication of this book is concrete evidence that the post-midlife years are a time to flourish in ways that we might never have imagined. My hope is that this book encourages us all to redefine this stage in life where new surprises and imaginings are possible.

1   The Need for a New Outlook

It's not how old you are, it's how you are old.

(Anonymous)

Only privileged individuals are allowed to grow old. For those who are fortunate enough to age, life can be a gift in which one can bask in nature, the company of close friends and family, and chosen passions and interests. Nonetheless, the aging process can be daunting in a society that glorifies youth, physical beauty, productivity, and efficiency. The slow progression of loss often associated with the aging process is often difficult to endure. Loss of one's young self, diminishing physicality, and eventually the loss of loved ones comes with great heartache. The unknown author's words above are pertinent for these reasons. The challenge in later life is how to glean meaning and purpose in life in spite of the obstacles in the aging process. In other words, how can older adults gather and harvest the fruits of experience?

The purpose of this book is to expand our thinking on what it means for women post-midlife to age in our society today. The ideas and conclusions drawn here are based on interviews with women between the ages of 63 and 73 who shared their stories and reflections, joys and tribulations about this developmental life stage. The interviews focused on how women "live through" life after many of the goals and tasks of earlier adulthood have already been met and accomplished. Prior to delving into these women's lived experience, however, it is important to look at where we currently stand as a society in relation to the aging process. It is only through understanding the process of aging in the past and the present that we can entertain ideas about redefining the future and answering the question of how individuals can create and maintain meaning in their lives post-midlife.

2 The Need for a New Outlook

Lifespan Demographics

What does it mean to be old? People are now living longer than previous generations and older adults compose a much larger segment of the population than ever before. In 1935, life expectancy was 61.7 years old and people could start collecting pension checks at age 62.[1] Lifespan demographics have changed dramatically in the ensuing years. According to a report published on October 8, 2014, by the Centers for Disease Control and Prevention, a typical toddler born in 2012 can expect to live 78.8 years.[2] Further, projected life expectancy by the mid-century in developed countries will be 82 years.[3] In light of longer life spans, the idea that a person passes directly from post-midlife to old age is being re-evaluated. Sociologists, entrepreneurs, and demographers have called for envisioning a new stage of life beyond midlife to serve as a bridge between midlife and old age.[4] As a matter of nomenclature, "The Third Chapter," "The Third Age," and "The Encore Stage," have been proposed as monikers for identifying a time in life when a person is neither old nor young.[5] This renaming and redefining of the later period of life recognizes that society has held on to an outdated idea that post-midlife is a time of relaxation and leisure. Twenty years of indolence seems healthy for neither the economy nor for individuals' physical and mental health. It is the task of this book to seek to understand how individuals post-midlife can create meaningful and productive penultimate acts.

Current Social Perspectives on Aging

Late life, covering a span of over three decades following age 50, can be perceived and understood in many different ways.[6] This period can be defined by physical appearance, key life events (e.g., retirement or some other disengagement) or social roles (e.g., grandparenthood or elder statesman duties). Later life has also been divided by some demographers and gerontologists into two different subgroups: the "young old" and the "old old."[7] Due to the high variability of individuals in later life, it is difficult to make general statements and assumptions about this portion of the population. Further, the highly complex nature surrounding patterns of aging makes it difficult to generalize about the process of aging and its effects on contemporary life. An overview of the social issues surrounding aging reveals that the current wide scope does not completely address the heterogeneity of this population nor the myriad of social policies that deserve attention.

Social policy analysts are being asked to examine issues around aging more carefully in light of demographic aging—an increase in the population that is 65 years and older. Based on the demographic data, global aging has expanded throughout the world.[8] In the United States, older persons (i.e., 65+ years) included 39.6 million individuals in 2009, representing 12.9% of the population or one in every eight Americans.[9] By 2030, demographers predict that there will be approximately 72.1 million older persons, more than twice their number in 2000.[10] By 2050 this age segment is predicted to number over 88.5 million adults.[11] This steady increase in the older adult population in the United States and the world at large will result in significant implications that will affect many social policy domains: the general economy, the healthcare system, the need for housing, and the general welfare of the individual older adult.[12]

The General Economy

Traditionally, societies supported older people via a system of intergenerational reciprocity.[13] In the family system, adults provide for young children, and, when these children grow up, they often care for their older parents. This support system extends from the family unit to society at large: Adults in the labor market subsidize the public programs that provide health care and income support for older dependents and health care and education for younger ones.[14] This intergenerational reciprocity functions optimally when birth cohorts generate enough "working age" adults to support both the younger and older members of society.[15] In most of Europe, North America, and Asia, there is a steady decrease in the number of working age people available to support older adults, a number that is predicted to continue to decline due to decreased fertility rates.[16] China, for example, is particularly concerned about its dependency ratio and is considering a change in the 36-year-old one child law in which families will be allowed to have two children.[17] If the new policy takes effect, experts warn that it will take decades to relieve the demographic crisis.

In addition to this challenging dependency ratio, the budgetary needs for older adults have increased with the growing number of adults living longer.[18] Thus, contemporary society faces a shrinking pool of younger workers being asked to support a larger pool of older retirees over a longer period of time.[19] However, these unfavorable dependency ratios are not seen as dire by all health service researchers.[20] For example, Knickman and Snell cite statistics demonstrating that the United States prospered through the 1960s with dependency ratios less favorable than will be experienced in 2030, and that the demographic disparity did not overwhelm the economy.

Kulik et al. working on their hypothesis that the economy may be burdened by the growing older population, suggest two possible solutions to address this quandary:

4   *The Need for a New Outlook*

1   Redefine "working age" and retain older people in the workforce for a longer period.
2   Boost immigration to increase the volume of "working-age" people.

Redefining "working age" is seen as a possibility given that longer life expectancy means that people can work beyond the time that is currently seen as the retirement period. In Australia, for example, there are plans to incrementally increase the official retirement age to 70 by 2035, making its retirement age the highest in the world.[21] There are many supporting and opposing views regarding these suggestions, including whether they would create more financial woes for society at large.[22]

A problem that exists with retaining people in the workforce for longer periods is the issue of discrimination against older workers in the workplace.[23] Despite research showing no performance differences between older and younger employees, discrimination is seen in both the work environment itself and hiring practices.[24] According to a U.S. Equal Employment Opportunity Commission report, in 2010, nationwide filings of workplace discrimination charges reached an unprecedented high.[25] Once unemployed, older individuals remain out of work, on average, longer than their younger counterparts.[26] Thus, while there are various predictions regarding how an older population will affect the general economy, it seems prudent for researchers and social policy analysts to continue to explore the best means to prevent older adults from becoming a burden to the next generation. One necessary step towards this goal is tackling the issue of ageism.

The Healthcare System

Demographic aging is often viewed as a phenomenon with increasing importance because of direct implications for healthcare.[27] A common assumption is that population aging would inevitably lead to significantly increased expenditure in health services.[28] Nonetheless, not everyone in the field supports this assumption. Specifically, a study in the U.S. showed that medical costs increased eight times between 1940 and 1990;[29] upon further investigation, however, the study showed that demographic aging only explained approximately 15% of the total increase.[30] Other factors, such as the development of new and expensive technologies, played a much more significant role in the rise of healthcare costs during this time interval. Therefore, while health care cost will rise with population aging, it is possible that the increase will be more manageable than unreflective extrapolation would predict.

Others also were not alarmed by the increase in healthcare expenses suggesting that "the burden of aging in 2030 should be no greater than the

The Need for a New Outlook 5

economic burden associated with raising large numbers of baby boom children in the 1960's."[31] These authors advocate four changes to offset growing medical expenses associated with population aging:

1. creating a working finance system for long-term care;
2. building a viable and affordable community-based delivery system;
3. investing in healthy aging in order to achieve lower disability rates; and
4. reinvigorating the concept of family and the value of seniors in American culture.[32]

Long-Term Care

Long-term care is one of the most expensive healthcare costs associated with an aging population.[33] This type of care includes a broad continuum of services that address the needs of people who require help with activities of everyday living.[34] These services can be delivered by family and friends or by the formal services of home care, assisted living facilities, or nursing homes.[35] The Congressional Budget Office (CBO) estimated that expenditures on formal long-term care totaled more than $120 billion in 2000, with 59% of all expenses covered by the public sector. Conservative estimates from CBO suggest that formal long-term care expenditures will increase to $270 billion in 2030. These figures translate into an increasing pressure on Medicare and Medicaid to finance an ever-increasing aging population. In 1995, over 64% of elderly nursing home residents used Medicaid to finance at least some of their care.[36] In New York, records showed that the Medicaid programs paid for 80% of all nursing home costs.[37] Given this data, Knickman and Snell urge social policy analysts to direct their attention to improving the financing of long-term care. One possibility Knickman and Snell advance is instituting a mandatory insurance plan, along the lines of today's (September, 2017) mandatory medical insurance, to prevent long-term insurance from becoming an overwhelming public burden.[38]

Community-Based Care

To meet the growing demands of an aging population, it is crucial to develop a viable and affordable community-based delivery system.[39] Researchers describe three stages of aging to help guide community planning: the healthy-active phase, the slowing down phase, and the service-needy phase.[40] According to these authors, at the first stage, when elders are healthy and active, the community must learn how to tap the human resources that elders can provide. Seniors can be key volunteers to improve

6 The Need for a New Outlook

the life of many segments of society. Additionally, healthy, active seniors can be considered a potential component of the paid workforce if jobs can be structured to meet their preferences and capabilities.

The authors further suggested that during the second stage, when elders begin to slow down, dependable, affordable transportation systems need to be in place. The availability of transportation can help with the further growth of seniors' ability to serve as volunteers—an important community need for elders at this stage to ensure that they continue to feel socially connected, active, and engaged. In order to grow volunteerism, communities need to recruit, train, and support older adult volunteers in order to make volunteerism a viable service.[41]

Lastly, for the service-needy stage, formal care must be better structured at the community level. Communities must provide training and respite programs to assist friends and family caregivers who care for older adults in residential settings. Financial support for these volunteer caregivers should also be considered so as not to develop an overreliance on institutional settings. Additionally, communities must develop formal community-based services for those who are frail and in need of more care in order to avoid too much reliance on nursing homes. These new models would include adult day services and housing-based services that can use one caregiver to assist more than one older adult at a time. Moving away from the traditional one-on-one model can make community long-term care a more affordable option. Thus, community-based care calls upon all of society to address the needs of older adults in a more socially inclusive manner.[42] These expansions in community care for elders need to be given political priority and financial resources in order to help offset the high price of formal long-term care.

Investing in Healthy Aging

Keeping seniors healthy and functioning could produce significant economic value.[43] Despite the focus on healthy aging, some members of society seem to be more vulnerable and in need of more preventative care. These members demonstrate health inequalities in later life related to wealth and social position.[44] Additionally, research has shown that education exerts a significant effect on both health status and health services.[45] These findings point to the need for outreach to older adult members of society regardless of income and education.

Cultural Attitudes

The idea of elders as an economic burden or as frail and weak is an outdated construct.[46] A new image for aging is necessary, in which elders are

The Need for a New Outlook 7

seen as assets with an important role to play in society.[47] This cultural shift could help with age integration such that all members of society, regardless of age, have something to contribute to the whole.[48] Additionally, when older adults become less prone to social isolation and feelings of worthlessness, their medical and emotional health greatly improves.[49]

The Need for Housing

Housing problems arise from the fact that residential needs and demands change as a natural consequence of aging.[50] The issue of where and how elders are going to live is becoming increasingly pressing. When elders begin to slow down in regard to their work and social activity as well as family functioning, smaller housing units that are more aging-friendly but still affordable must be integrated in the community.[51] The idea of "aging in place," in which seniors stay in their own homes and communities, is becoming an increasingly popular alternative.[52] Bookman documents three new models for aging-in-place: naturally occurring retirement communities (NORCs), villages, and campus-affiliated residences. These models could serve as templates on how to design communities, both physically and socially, to support the needs of an aging population.

NORCs are housing developments that were not planned or designed for older people but which, over time, come to house largely older people.[53] In certain cities within the United States over 50% of the residents are elderly as a result of adults staying in their homes long after their children have grown.[54] This phenomenon could be the basis for innovations in the delivery of care and housing for older adults. The process reflects a reaction to a naturally occurring phenomenon, which further translates into an intentional community of elders.[55] Today the term NORC is used to mean a conscious attempt to develop and offer elder services in an area where there is a high concentration of older adults. The first NORC with supportive service programs was the Penn South Houses Program (NORC-SSP) in New York City, developed in 1985.[56] Currently there are NORC-SSP programs in 25 American states that are part of the National NORC's Aging in Place Initiative organized by the United Jewish Communities.[57] In New York state alone, 41 sites have adopted this model.[58] Their key components include:

1   A key geographical location where many elders live in close proximity to each other. NORCs are most commonly found in urban areas.
2   A multi-generational, age-integrated building, or neighborhood that encourages younger residents to interact with older residents.
3   Some level of involvement of elders in the planning of services and activities.

8 The Need for a New Outlook

4   NORC, with the help of social service agencies, contracts with local service providers who can deliver home care, transportation, and health care providers. NORCs can also partner with schools and businesses to make services more available and affordable.

5   Residents are organized to provide tasks or services to each other on a volunteer basis.

The second model to emerge as an alternative to traditional housing for elders is the "village" model.[59] This model connects people aged 50 and older with supportive services. A village offers its fee-paying members preferred access to social and cultural activities, health and fitness programs, household and home maintenance services, medical care and transportation. The goal of the village is to provide members all the assets found in an independent or assisted living facility without requiring them to move from their homes. There are now 12–14 such villages operating and 10 others that have used one or more elements of the model to create their own alternatives.[60]

The third aging-in-place model connects elders to institutions of higher education. It is estimated that the campuses of approximately 80 colleges and universities now include housing integrated with life-long learning options for seniors.[61] There are three basic components within this model:

1   An academic emphasis in which elders can enroll in courses.

2   A health care emphasis in which independent living, assisted living, long-term care facilities, and hospice are available.

3   A real estate emphasis in which developers and builders worked in tandem with the college or university.

Additionally, residents have access to the cultural programs, recreational facilities, and medical facilities on campus. One of the leaders in developing this type of community is Lasell College in Massachusetts.[62] That institution requires all Lasell Village residents to pursue 450 hours of study per year under the supervision of a full-time dean. The participation of the "villagers" gives students and elders valuable time to interact and learn from each other. This village also houses the Rosemary B. Fuss Center for Research on Aging and Intergenerational Studies that connects villagers and Lasell full-time students in research and teaching focused on aging issues.[63] One of the key elements in these three models (i.e., NORCs, villages, and campus-affiliated residences) is the idea that elders are active participants who are expected to be engaged in building a caring society through reciprocity and engagement in civic and social life. These aging-in-place initiatives share a commitment to keeping elders out of

The Need for a New Outlook 9

institutional settings and in their own homes. Several of the NORC-SSPs exist in subsidized housing complexes. The Villages and campus-affiliated communities are located in fairly affluent neighborhoods. This raises the question whether aging-in-place organizations can be developed in moderate-income neighborhoods for residents who do not have disposable income but have too much income for subsidized services. How communities organize elder care and housing has repercussions for people of all ages.[64] These new models seem to offer a higher quality of living for older adults while at the same time keeping economic costs down for all of society.[65]

The Individual

Gerontologists maintain that negative and often ageist attitudes lie at the root of the worst problems that can affect older people.[66] Negative stereotypes have the power to damage social and personal identities.[67] The media are one source that perpetuates these negative stereotypes.[68] The media exclude the images of older adults in favor of the 18–49 demographic.[69] Further, when older adults are depicted in the media, it is often a negative portrayal of physical and mental decline, unattractiveness and loss of independence.[70] Coupland concluded that advertising depicts older adults as undesirable and conveys a message that older adult consumers must either assume the responsibility of staying young-looking or must disguise physical aging in order to remain attractive to society.[71] This glorification of youth creates a challenge for adults in later life to maintain their self-esteem at the same time that their bodies and minds undergo the natural aging process.

Negative age stereotypes exist within social media sites also. Content analysis of publicly accessible Facebook groups found that descriptions about the old focused on negative age stereotypes.[72] Results showed 74% of the descriptions excoriated the old, 41% referred to physical debilitation, 27% to cognitive debilitation, and 13% to both types of debilitation. An example of excoriating the old, read as follows:

> Old people do not contribute to modern society at all. Their single and only meaning is to nag and to moan. Therefore, any Old Age Pensioner that passes the age of 69 should immediately face a firing squad.[73]

Another example of a description that was categorized as presenting cognitive and physical debilitation read:

> Old people are a pain in the (expletive deleted) as far as I'm concerned and they are a burden on society. I hate everything about them,

10 *The Need for a New Outlook*

from their hair nets in the rain to their white Velcro sneakers. They are cheap, they smell like (expletive deleted) ... they are senile, they complain about everything, they couldn't hear a dumptruck ...[74]

Levy, Chung, Bedford, and Navrazhina advance the idea that Facebook should provide a buffer from this type of hate speech by including protection for older adults by including them in their Community Standards, which notify all users not to "single out individuals based on race, ethnicity, national origin, religion, sex, gender, sexual orientation, disability or disease."[75] Levy, Chung, Bedford, and Navrazhina are concerned that, while social media has the potential to break down barriers between the generations, it may in fact be erecting new barriers by not having these protections in place.

In addition to ageism found in traditional and social media, negative stereotypes also result from Western society's value on "productiveness and effectiveness."[76] This myopic view of productivity, however, ignores the contribution elders can make to society by supporting each other and by supporting family and community.[77] This view further underlies an idea that aging is a slow and painful deterioration and decline towards death.[78] This orientation loses sight of any redeemable positive gains that accompany growing old.[79]

Negative stereotypes of older adults can also be understood through the lens of terror management theory.[80] From this perspective, Martens et al. posit that negative attitudes and behaviors directed towards elderly people can be explained in large part by people's own fears about aging and death. Accordingly, at the core of ageism is the fear people have to die, face their physicality, and suffer loss.[81] The elderly, under these circumstances, become reminders of these threats.[82] According to these authors, society must face these threats of mortality directly or develop more enduring defenses against them in order to combat ageism.

Once these stereotypes have been embedded in our thinking, they become powerful forces in the way society operates. Angus spoke about the myths of aging and the stereotypes that develop in their wake:

Myths most commonly relate to progressive physical and mental decline, social isolation, asexual behavior, lack of creativity, and economic and familial burden. Older people are frequently labeled as a dependent liability, a social problem constructed around the concept of dependency and how to prevent it. Furthermore, the more influential the group doing the labeling, the more widespread is the acceptance of this largely unquestioned ageist stereotype and the interests it serves.[83]

The Need for a New Outlook 11

Angus amplifies this idea by explaining the ripple effect of these stereotypes and how they come to "permeate organizations, inform policy, act as social determinants of health, and have the power to shift attention from individual experiences and social conditions."[84] Consequently, society's attitude towards its aging population is an issue that needs more attention and focus in order to move forward in a positive fashion.

This brief overview of lifespan demographics and current social perspectives on aging points to an intricate web of interconnected public issues: the economy, the healthcare system, the need for appropriate housing, and the detrimental cultural attitudes towards older adults. However, what emerges clearly within this maze of social issues, is that society is being called on to give more conscious attention to this segment of society and develop a new outlook regarding the post-midlife years. With people living longer lives it is incumbent on our society to find ways to empower older adults so that they continue to be contributors to society as long as possible.

Notes

1 Irving, 2014.
2 Xu, Kochanek, Murphy, & Arias, 2014.
3 Lavretsky, Sajatovic, & Reynolds III, 2013.
4 Freedman, 2011; Laslett, 1989; Lawrence-Lightfoot, 2009.
5 Lawrence-Lightfoot, 2009; Laslett, 1989; Freedman, 2011.
6 Lloyd-Sherlock, 2000.
7 Baltes & Smith, 2003; Garfein & Herzog, 1995; Lloyd-Sherlock, 2000.
8 Bloom, Canning, & Fink, 2010; Evans & Niederehe, 2013; Frankenberg & Thomas, 2011; Irving, 2014; Kinsella & Phillips, 2005; Lloyd-Sherlock, 2000.
9 Administration on Aging, 2014.
10 Ibid.
11 Evan & Niederehe, 2013.
12 Bengtson & Lowenstein, 2003; Bloom et al., 2010; DaVanzo, 2001; Kinsella & Phillips, 2005; Kochera, Straight, & Guterbock, 2005; Kulik, Ryan, Harper, & George, 2014; United Nations, 2013.
13 Becker, Beyene, Newsom, & Mayen, 2003; Kinsella & Phillips, 2005; Kulik et al., 2014.
14 Bloom et al., 2010; Börsch-Supan, 2003; Kulik et al., 2014; Tosun, 2003; United Nations, 2013.
15 Bloom et al., 2010; Kulik et al., 2014; United Nations, 2013.
16 Bloom et al., 2010; Börsch-Supan, 2003; Kulik et al., 2014; Tosun, 2003; United Nations, 2013.
17 Winsor, 2015.
18 Kulik et al., 2014; United Nations, 2013.
19 Kulik et al., 2014; United Nations, 2013.
20 Caplan, 2011; Futagami & Nakajima, 2001; Knickman & Snell, 2002.
21 Kulik et al., 2014, p. 930.

12 *The Need for a New Outlook*

22 Bloom et al., 2010; Börsch-Supan, 2003; Futagami & Nakajima, 2001; Tosun, 2003.
23 Malinen & Johnston, 2013; Mermin, Johnson, & Toder, 2008.
24 Malinen & Johnston, 2013.
25 Perry & Wolburg, 2011.
26 Ibid.
27 Centers for Disease Control and Prevention, 2003; Congressional Budget Office, 1999; DaVanzo, 2001; Frankenberg & Thomas, 2011; Kinsella & Phillips, 2005; Knickman & Snell, 2002; Lloyd-Sherlock, 2000; van der Gaag & Precker, 1997.
28 Centers for Disease Control and Prevention, 2003.
29 van der Gaag & Precker, 1997.
30 Ibid.
31 Knickman & Snell, 2002, p. 849.
32 Knickman & Snell, 2002.
33 Congressional Budget Office, 1999; Knickman & Snell, 2002.
34 Congressional Budget Office, 1999; Knickman & Snell, 2002.
35 Congressional Budget Office, 1999; Knickman & Snell, 2002.
36 Knickman & Snell, 2002.
37 Ibid.
38 The Affordable Care Act may be revised by the current administration.
39 Knickman & Snell, 2002; Kochera et al., 2005.
40 Knickman & Snell, 2002.
41 Ibid.
42 Bookman, 2008; Kochera et al., 2005; Morgan, 2014.
43 Centers for Disease Control and Prevention, 2003; Kochera et al., 2005.
44 Lloyd-Sherlock, 2000.
45 Ibid.
46 Knickman & Snell, 2002; Kochera et al., 2005.
47 Bookman, 2008; Morgan, 2014; Yeh, 2015.
48 Bookman, 2008; Kochera et al., 2005; Morgan, 2014; Yeh, 2015.
49 Bookman, 2008; Kochera et al., 2005.
50 Bookman, 2008; Folts & Muir, 2002; Kinsella & Phillips, 2005; Kochera et al., 2005; Matthews & Turnbull, 2008; Smith, Rayer, Smith, Wang, & Zeng, 2012.
51 Kochera et al., 2005; Matthews & Turnbull, 2008.
52 Bookman, 2008; Morgan, 2014.
53 Bookman, 2008; Morgan, 2014.
54 Bookman, 2008.
55 Ibid.
56 Ibid.
57 Ibid.
58 Ibid.
59 Ibid.
60 Ibid.
61 Ibid.
62 Ibid.
63 Ibid.
64 Bookman, 2008; Folts & Muir, 2002; Kinsella & Phillips, 2005; Kochera et al., 2005; Matthews & Turnbull, 2008; Smith et al., 2012.
65 Bookman, 2008.

The Need for a New Outlook   13

66 Angus, 2006.
67 Angus, 2006; Calasanti, 2005; Coupland, 2007; Perry & Wolburg, 2011; Yeh, 2015.
68 Perry & Wolburg, 2011.
69 Ibid.
70 Ibid.
71 Coupland, 2007.
72 Levy, Chung, Bedford, & Navrazhina, 2014.
73 Levy, Chung, Bedford, & Navrazhina, 2014, p. 173.
74 Levy, Chung, Bedford, & Navrazhina, 2014, pp. 173–174.
75 Levy, Chung, Bedford, & Navrazhina, 2014, pp. 172–173.
76 Angus, 2006, p. 138.
77 Yeh, 2015.
78 Ibid.
79 Coupland, 2007; Yeh, 2015.
80 Martens et al., 2005.
81 Calasanti, 2005.
82 Ibid.
83 Angus, 2006, p. 139.
84 Angus, 2006, pp. 139–140.

2 How We Age

Theories and Research

With the goal of developing a new outlook regarding the post-midlife years, it is essential to look at theories and research regarding aging. At the outset, it should be stated that there are many voices, within the medical, gerontology, and psychology fields, that contribute to the discussion of the aging process. There are times that these distinct disciplines work in tandem and other times that they seem to ignore important aspects of aging. The medical model, for example, often focuses on the biological properties of aging while ignoring the mind and soul. Although the ideal would be an integrated approach, the current presentation is an attempt to share the scholarly body of knowledge that is currently available.

Successful Aging

In the past two decades, many studies have investigated aging under the all-purpose heading of "successful aging."[1] The models differ, however, in their definition and conceptualization of the construct of "successful aging." For Rowe and Kahn, the definition of successful aging included three components: low probability of disease and disease-related disability, high cognitive and physical functional capacity, and active engagement with life. Schulz and Heckhausen equated successful aging with the development and maintenance of primary control throughout the life course. In other words, individuals who are able to engage and impact the environments around them for the longest period of time would be judged most successful. Ryff postulated a multidimensional approach that based successful aging on six criteria: self-acceptance, positive relations with others, autonomy, environmental mastery, purpose in life, and personal growth. Baltes and Baltes offered yet another schema, in which successful aging was evaluated in terms of personal goal attainment, the minimization of losses, and the maximization of gains.[2] Of these models,

How We Age   15

the Baltes and Baltes model has been received best and withstood the least criticism.[3] Nonetheless, there is no general consensus about what constitutes successful aging.

Researchers involved in predicting successful aging have looked to operationalize the successful aging construct in order to yield quantifiable data and add their findings to the knowledge base.[4] Morgan et al. found that routine physical activity was a significant predictor of well-being for men but not for women. Jorm et al. found that predictors for successful aging were higher educational level and occupational status in men, younger age in women, lower neuroticism in women, non-smoking in women, and higher verbal intelligence in both men and women. Successful aging was defined as having good to excellent health, no disabilities in activities of daily living, good cognitive functioning, and living in the community. Garfein and Herzog found that greater social contact, better health, better vision, and fewer stressful life events were reliable predictors of successful aging. In summary, several of these empirical studies have identified that one can successfully age by … not aging and the contradiction is blatant. Reker explains that:

> With advancing age these resource domains are prone to increasing instability, shrinkage and eventual loss, leading to a reduction in the individual's capacity for optimal adaptation. Since losses cannot be reversed, we need to begin to identify substitute resources that can stabilize and augment the aging individual's resource potential. An individual's existential belief system may be one of a number of substitute resources that could fill the void.[5]

Reker's words are an invitation to look at "successful aging" from a different vantage point given that physical decline is known to occur decades prior to the end of life. His ideas suggest that humans can continue to find purpose and meaning in their later years through inner resources that are not solely dependent upon biological and physical states of being. In summary, instead of focusing on retaining control over physical functioning as a means to age well, other existential variables deserve attention that may contribute to a purposeful and meaningful life in the later years.

Existential Perspectives and Aging

An extensive and established tradition in psychology scholarship has focused on exploring the meaning of human existence.[6] These thinkers developed thoughtful and perceptive theories about the purpose and

16 *How We Age*

meaning of life. Concepts related to Jung's Individuation, Frankl's Will to Meaning, Maslow's Self-Actualization, and Rogers' Fully Functioning Person have advanced knowledge and understanding of what it means to be human. Their ideas are steeped in the world of clinical studies and critical thinking; although the concepts are theoretically complex, several theoreticians have applied these concepts to the aging process.

Generativity

The concept of generativity is derived from Erik Erikson's developmental theory.[7] Erikson saw personality as a life-long developmental process made up of eight distinct psychosocial stages spanning from birth through late life. (Erikson's wife, Joan Erikson, added a ninth stage to this theory as a result of watching her husband grow old.)[8] In Erikson's developmental model, successfully negotiating and mastering each stage is a prerequisite to advancing to the next stage. Each stage strengthens the self and allows for greater maturity. Erikson's formulation takes epigenesis as its model, a term obtained from embryology.[9] Epigenesis refers to the *unfolding* development in an organism as seen in the development of a plant or an animal.[10] According to Erikson's theory personality *unfolds* within the human organism in eight predetermined stages that are characterized by a defining issue or crisis.[11] The interplay between biological pressures and factors within the social and cultural environment is the driving force behind each stage's defining issue or crisis.[12]

Erikson's seventh developmental stage is Generativity versus Stagnation. The focus of this stage is to nurture, guide, and ensure the well-being of future generations and leave a lasting legacy. Current theorists and researchers propose that generativity plays a significant role in the final decades of life.[13] Villar draws upon Erikson's later writings when he adopted the term of *grand generativity* to explain the helping and supportive activities of older people. Villar suggests that generativity applies beyond midlife today due to new generations who enter older age being better educated and living longer. Villar suggests that, in order to test this framework, more research is needed. He enumerates the needed clarifications as:

1 Understanding which factors trigger or encourage generativity in older age.
2 Understanding developmental implications of generativity and how generativity changes during older age.
3 Understanding how generative objectives and motives are adjusted to adapt to changing abilities throughout the lifespan.

How We Age   17

Glass et al., analyzed a program named Experience Corps in terms of its ability to create or increase generativity in older adults.[14] Experience Corps was designed in 1993–1995 by Linda Fried and Marc Freedman.[15] The program involved the recruitment, training, and deployment of older adults to volunteer time and experience in underserved elementary schools. The program was designed to help older adults, schools, and the broader community. Glass et al., concluded that there is evidence that the program met the generativity needs of its volunteers based upon the high program retention rates, with 80% of volunteers returning each year. Limitations of the study, however, were that the program attracted a selective, high functioning, and small subset of the older population. The authors of this report also expressed the need for more research in order to better understand how older adults can be generative by expanding their care towards others via passing on wisdom and knowledge to the generations that follow in their footsteps.

Warburton, McLaughlin, and Pinsker designed a qualitative research study to explore whether community involvement in later life provides a greater sense of generativity.[16] Qualitative data, collected through focus group interviews, were analyzed interpretively using recent developments in Erikson's theory of generativity as a framework. Findings from the study provided important empirical evidence to illustrate generativity in relation to a sample of older Australians. The respondents in the study indicated that their lives had been enriched by generative behaviors that, for them, had contributed to a positive experience of aging.

Much remains unknown regarding how Erikson's developmental stage of Generativity vs. Stagnation gets played out in real life. Given the increase in older adults over the last decades coupled with their greater activity and health levels, it behooves society to understand how older adults can access and enhance generativity.[17]

Quest for Meaning

Viktor Frankl postulated that there is a human motive to seek purpose and meaning in our lives.[18] He theorized that people are more than biological, social, and psychological beings in that they have a spiritual element that drives them to find ultimate meaning during their existence. Further, Frankl proposed that there is a defiant power in the human spirit that can transcend the detrimental effects of stressful situations, illness, or the influence of the past. Frankl developed the therapeutic practice of logotherapy as a means to help patients find meaning in their lives. Further, several scales, such as the Purpose in Life Test (PIL) and the Meaning Life Questionnaire (MLQ) have based their constructs upon Frankl's theory of meaning.[19]

18   *How We Age*

Some investigators maintain that this existential need to draw a sense of meaning from one's existence plays a larger role in the lives of older people.[20] Martens et al. draw upon "terror theory" to argue that unconscious concerns about death enhance the need to view the world as a meaningful place. This view is intricately linked with Frankl's ideas, as Frankl developed his theory against the backdrop of his personal terror in a Nazi concentration camp. Frankl's experiences as an inmate led him to discover the importance of finding meaning in all forms of existence, even the most brutal ones.

During Frankl's later years, he spoke directly about how his theory related to the aging process.[21] Frankl argued that the crisis of old age is a crisis of meaning. If one sees aging simply through a biological lens, then the process is filled with losses. Frankl maintained that the challenge is to keep the lenses diverse such that wisdom and not biology becomes the primary focus, as wisdom is the real essence of being human. From this wider perspective, Frankl claimed that aging adults must be lifted and re-humanized to enable them to see themselves as greater than their losses. To reach this higher level, Frankl asserted that the older adult must see himself as both physical and beyond physical, at the same time. Wisdom can play a part in this transforming sense of self in old age as a means to discern the difference between the core part of the self and the peripheral part of self. The process of creating a coherent concept of self requires the older adult to reach beyond "what they have" to "what they truly are."[22]

Recent studies looking at therapeutic interventions aimed at increasing existential meaning in the lives of older adults have showed successful results.[23] Zanjiran et al. conducted 10 sessions of group logotherapy with older women residents within a nursing home. The findings of this study showed that group logotherapy significantly decreased the sense of loneliness in the experimental group. Malette and Oliver designed a qualitative study to explore whether and how "Life Review" can facilitate adjustment to retirement. Life Review (LR) refers to the process of looking back to the past in order to inform and bring meaning to the present. LR can use various techniques such as personal story-telling, oral history, reminiscence, guided autobiography, life history interviewing, and structured life review. In Malette and Oliver's study, participants were asked to reminisce on memories that touched upon the themes of strengths and life goals and explore how these areas could be reconciled with retirement. Results suggested that LR can facilitate the retirement process by helping individuals' search for existential meaning. These two studies[24] in conjunction with research pointing to meaning-making playing a larger role in the lives of older people[25] serve as confirmation of Frankl's ideas. The importance of older adults overcoming their losses and focusing on an enlarged meaning of themselves appears to be a key to aging well.

Individuation

Carl Jung discussed the second half of life as a time when a person becomes more ready for individuation—a process that facilitates individuals developing beyond their ego states and incorporating into consciousness other powerful internal structures of the personal and collective unconscious.[26] Whereas the first half of life is governed by expansion of experience and adaptation to outer reality (i.e., personal relationships and the world of work), Jung theorized that the second half of life is characterized by greater engagement with philosophical and spiritual issues (i.e., values, creative endeavors and the search for life's meaning). Jung envisioned maturation as a life-long process and considered it a tragedy that many people live their entire lives with the erroneous idea that only during the first half of life do we develop and mature. According to Sawin, Jung viewed old age as:

> A summons to internal growth and personal development, and it provided the opportunity to enrich life, deepen spirituality and define a new sense of purpose or meaning. He wrote that we would not live to old age if longevity had no meaning for the species. Hence the later part of life must have an inherent significance.[27]

Jung's ideas about individuation and the second half of life have found a place in current theories and research regarding aging.[28] Tornstam's gerotranscendence theory suggested that as people age, their view of the world and themselves shifts. This shift entails a move away from a materialistic and pragmatic view to a more cosmic and transcendent view. This theory proposed that aging is a process of turning inwards through exploration of inner space, introspection, and deeper social relationships.

In quantitative studies, Tornstam found significant proportions of individuals aged 74 and older had changed and developed in the way they perceived themselves and their place in the world.[29] The concept of gerotranscendence was further validated in Tornstam's qualitative interviews with older adults.[30] In these interviews, Tornstam discovered that many older adults had increased life satisfaction in the context of a developmental pattern typically involving a redefinition of the self and relations to other people. Tornstam found that his informants described a process of transcending borders and barriers that had circumscribed them earlier in life. Specifically, these studies showed that individuals in later stages of life showed an increased affinity with others and with earlier generations, a sense of being part of a whole, a redefinition of time space, life, and death as well as an increased need for positive contemplative solitude.

20 How We Age

Further, Tornstam found an average increase in transcendence starting already in young adulthood. Tornstam revealed that in his research many older adults have reacted with recognition and relief when they learn about gerotranscendence, having noticed these qualities within themselves in contrast to socially maintained perspectives that aging is a series of losses rather than gains.[31] This concept was further recognized within popular culture: In August 2010, the *New York Times Health Blog* posted an article about gerotranscendence. Tornstam shared that he was struck by how many readers reacted with recognition and relief at learning about the concept.[32]

Studies from researchers have also revealed that gerotranscendence is related to coherence and life satisfaction.[33] Scarcello focused on perspectives of a distinct group of women 50 and over—those who perceived that life had become better and not worse with aging. Scarcello describes women in the study as "Women of Harvest" who, following their menopause, enter the "Open Fields," on which old barriers and borderlines could be transcended and wisdom harvested. von Humboldt et al. analyzed the indicators of adjustment to aging (AtA) and found that spirituality (i.e., dimension of gerotranscendence) was the most frequent indicator of AtA (43.2%) whereas economic situation was the least referred indicator of AtA (10.3%).

Building on Jung's legacy, contemporary Jungian scholars and practitioners also continued to contribute on the topic. The C. G. Jung Society of Washington D.C., in collaboration with the Library of Congress and the American Association of Retired Persons (AARP) Foundation, convened a symposium in 2012 entitled *Jung and Aging: Bringing to Life the Possibilities and Potentials for Vital Aging.*[34] The conference addressed Jung's ideas about on-going human development in the second half of life. In particular, the conference explored how society can change its views of aging from being a time of withdrawal and relentless decline to being a time of active engagement in and contribution to society. The scholars who presented at the conference envisioned the years beyond midlife as having the potential for being the most productive and satisfying periods in the human lifespan. Although acknowledging that the aging process holds many challenges around health, physical aging, and loss, the speakers envisioned this time period as also holding the potential for profound psychological and spiritual growth. In the process of exploring these issues, the conference highlighted and conceptualized significant variables that potentially shape the activity of meaning-making in the second half of life: Developmental Tasks, Spirituality, Relationships, Creativity, and Coming to Terms with Death.

How We Age 21

Developmental Tasks

Lionel Corbett further developed Jung's 1930s paper on *The Stages of Life* and identified five developmental tasks that are applicable to individuals in the second half of life.[35] They are as follows:

1 *The development of unused potential.* Due to the demands of work and family, individuals prior to midlife cannot actualize all of their potential. Therefore, individuals in the first half of life tend to experience that many aspects of their personality and creative talents are not allowed to flourish and must remain dormant. The second half of life offers time and energy to devote to talents that were not able to be fully cultivated at an earlier age.

2 *Type development.* Jung postulated that human beings have superior and inferior functions to personality depending on birth and lived experiences.[36] The theory is akin to always using the dominant hand due to preference and ease instead of developing strength in both hands. The thinking/feeling function refers to our preferred mode of making judgments in life and the sensation/intuition function is the preferred mode of gaining information.[37] Thus, the psychological functions that have never been developed may become important in later life. For example, the older person who is a feeling type and therefore adept at forming social relationships could develop the thinking function, by returning to school to study an area that has always been of interest but wasn't pursued due to lack of time. The person who tends to be intuitive and drawn to spiritual matters may choose to pursue and strengthen the sensate function by working manually, for example, in the form of gardening or painting.

3 *The development of the contrasexual aspects of the personality.* Jung described the life-long goal of individuation as a process of strengthening, differentiating, and integrating into consciousness the various non-ego parts of the psyche in order to obtain wholeness.[38] Towards this goal men are encouraged to integrate their unconscious feminine psychology (anima) and women to integrate their unconscious masculine psychology (animus). This process encourages men to mature and develop a more nurturing stance whereas women would experience more assertiveness and independence in order to achieve wholeness in the second half of life.

4 *Maintenance of self-esteem.* The second half of life requires a shift in the sources that promote self-esteem. Whereas life-long career achievements, financial success, raising a family, and athletic ability contribute to self-esteem in younger adulthood, these sources may

22 *How We Age*

become less available in later life. Adults in later adulthood must shift their focus to friendships, family, humor, wisdom, and one's fund of knowledge and life experience as new sources to promote self-esteem. The ability to accept the deficits and challenges of aging while clinging to the positive aspects of wisdom, maturity, and resiliency become the new tasks of later adulthood.

5   *New roles and responsibilities.* Late life offers different options in family, friendship, and community roles.

- *Family roles*: As people move on in age, a degree of role-reversal often follows as adult children take on the role of caregivers. The older adult must allow for mature dependence on others in order for this system to work. At the same time, however, the role of grandparent can become developmentally important for elders, adult children, and grandchildren.
- *Social roles:* As people age, they often lose those family and friends that are close to them. While these relationships can never be duplicated, it is important for the individual in the second half of life to retain the ability to form new friendships as a means to cope with a world that seems to be shrinking.
- *Civic roles*: Older adults whose time is no longer committed to externally defined pursuits but whose energies and abilities remain intact are in a special position to give back to society. Given their fund of knowledge, maturity, and experience, they are in a unique position to educate, lead, and help those that are less fortunate.

Spirituality

According to Jung, spirituality is at the center of the human developmental process.[39] Jung stated that:

The decisive question for man is: Is he related to something infinite or not? That is the telling question of his life. Only if we know that the thing that truly matters is the infinite can we avoid fixing our interests upon futilities, and upon all kinds of goals which are not of real importance. Thus, we demand that the world grant us recognition for qualities which we regard as personal possessions: our talent or our beauty. The more a man lays stress on false possessions, and the less sensitivity he has for what is essential, the less satisfying is his life. He feels limited because he has limited aims, and the result is envy and jealousy. If we understand and feel that here in this life we already

How We Age 23

have a link with the infinite, desires and attitudes change. In the final analysis, we count for something only because of the essential we embody, and if we do not embody that, life is wasted.[40]

Thus, Jung contributed to the conviction that psychological well-being is dependent upon personal engagement with the essential—in other words, with ultimate sources of meaning.[41] Costello advances this idea to propose that, without a renewal of purpose drawing from the "essential," aging in the second half of life can become a senseless waiting for the end of life. In order to meet the task of renewing meaning in later adulthood, a person must lead a soul-filled life that is spent in conversation with the stranger—the ever-emerging Self, a whole integrate sense of one's own self.[42] In the past, traditional religious practice filled this niche of connecting with ultimate sources of meaning. Today, however, there is a vacuum and Costello proposed that for many individuals "conscious aging" can be obtained by creating dialogue with the ever-emerging Self through "dream work, writing or reflection: through relating to the natural world as a subject rather than an object, creative works, attending to our emotions and the images that spring up out of the depths, as well as meaningful conversation, storytelling, prayer and ritual practices within or outside of a faith community."[43] Moreover, one of the primary features of spiritual development is the discovery of meaning in one's life.[44] For older adults, this is particularly important as a means to develop resiliency in the face of multiple losses and limitations, and to avoid the sense that one's life is defined by struggle and fate.

Relationships

Just as a flower needs the proper environment in order to blossom, Ruhl and Evans stated that humans need the supportive environment in order to bloom and reach their full potential.[45] The environment best suited for spiritual growth, meaning, and purpose is created within the powerful container of intimate and transformative relationships.[46] Ruhl and Evans maintained that, as people age, the need for enduring, supportive, and loving relationships becomes more urgent and is essential for well-being. Further, they suggested that "the research on aging shows categorically the physical and psychological benefits of intimate relationship: couples live richer, healthier, longer lives than singles."[47] These authors noted that it is not just relationship per se but rather the quality of the relationship that is the best predictor of health and well-being. The transformative relationship evolves within a stable long-term relationship in which both members take responsibility for their own inner work. Further, the relationship transcends a mature functional role in recognizing the spiritual and sacred aspects of

24 *How We Age*

the connection, according to Ruhl and Evans. It is interesting to note that Ruhl and Evans did not address the time in life when older adults may have lost significant and transcendent relationships due to illness and aging. Corbett has addressed this aspect, however, in underlining the developmental task of retaining the ability to form new friendships as a means to cope with a world that can appear to be shrinking.[48]

Creativity

Corbett amplified Jung's suggestion that the person who does not build will demolish and destroy, by emphasizing the essential need for creativity in older adults' lives as a path to psychological well-being and aliveness.[49] Similarly, Hanna described creativity as a vehicle that contributes to the individual's self-esteem and society's capacity to move forward. Hanna proposed three entry points to the engagement in creative expression or activities for older adults.[50]

1   *The beginning participant.* The beginning participant is the person who begins to have a desire to engage in creative expression later in life. This type of rebalancing or internal revelation is in keeping with Corbett's idea, described above, as *Type Development* in which a person with a strong intuitive function starts to strengthen their sensate function. Hanna maintained that many folk artists and untrained artists began art late in life as a means to express a story or image that they felt compelled to share.[51]

2   *The returning participant.* The returning participant is often one who has experienced a loss or change in life-status such as retirement, the death of a spouse or other family member, or the person's own encounter with illness. These people often were involved in creative pursuits when they were younger but discontinued these endeavors as job and family commitments took their time and energy. For older adults in this category, inviting creativity back into their lives is like welcoming an old friend who can bring joy, comfort, and a renewed sense of meaning and purpose.

3   *The life-long participant.* The life-long participant is an individual who has been immersed in creativity for most of their life. These older adults may be professional artists, scientists, or innovators in other fields. Individuals in this group were drawn to creative expression early in life and have defined who they are based on this way of being and perceiving the world. Life-long participants have often been identified as role models for successful aging as they often stay highly engaged in life and thereby do not lose their sense of purpose or meaning.

How We Age   25

Coming to Terms with Death

Contemporary Western society has a collective resistance to accepting death as part of the life cycle.[52] In the spirit of the Jungian tradition, Costello encouraged individuals to revisit myth and literature as a reminder that the path of refusing death always leads to tragedy. In the Greek myth of Tithonus, Eos, the goddess of the dawn, and Tithonus, a mortal, become lovers. Eos beseeches Zeus to make Tithonus immortal so that the couple can be together always but forgets to ask that Tithonus remain eternally youthful. Zeus grants Eos her wish but in the process subjects Tithonus to a fate worse than death—loss of his physical and mental capacities with no hope of death's release. Eos abandons Tithonus in this state by shutting him away in a golden chamber where his isolation is complete. This myth elucidates how the human tendency of running away from the laws of nature can only create further suffering.

A version of this same Greek myth is found in Alfred, Lord Tennyson's poem *Tithonus*.[53] In this version of the story, Tithonus makes the fateful request on his own behalf to Eos rather than Zeus. Tithonus in this rendition is tormented as his unnatural condition separates him from his human community. Tithonus's immortality robs him of his true self and symbolically kills him. Tithonus longs to be resting peacefully underground with his long-gone fellows—the "happier dead."

These two versions of the Tithonus myth may be viewed as a lesson to those who might try to hold onto life longer than the natural order dictates. In terms of finding meaning in the second half of life, it seems self-evident that the idea of grabbing onto unlived potential only makes sense within the context of beginnings, endings, and transformations within those parameters. Therefore, society and individuals in the second half of life may benefit from viewing death as a natural and necessary part of the lifecycle.

Other Voices from the Jungian Tradition

Hollis comes to the subject of finding meaning in the second half of life from a different standpoint.[54] For Hollis, much of earlier adulthood is a process of adaptation and adjustment to others' expectations as a means to efficiently raise family, develop careers, and to generally make one's place in the world. In contrast, the second half of life is a time to develop one's authentic self: a time to soften the voices of authority figures and listen instead to the more personal voice of the soul. Hollis depicts the second half of life as a time to risk in order to serve "life not death, growth not aversive adaptation."[55]

26 *How We Age*

Hollis has formulated four questions that those in the second half of life must ask themselves as a means to enlarge their thinking, spark their curiosity, and retain a sense of purpose and meaning.[56]

1   *Where has fear blocked my development, kept me constricted, and still prevents me from being who I am?* Having spent the first half of life in a state of adaptation, individuals in the second half of life often fall into a pattern in which they are defined by strategies of conflict avoidance. At this life stage, however, it is essential for older adults to ask themselves how they have let themselves down due to fear or just not "showing up." This type of honest soul-searching often results in recovering an interest, talent, or enthusiasm left behind. It might also mean "risking doing what you wish to do with your precious time and energy whether it fits in with others, whether it is approved by others, and whether it is difficult or not."[57]

2   *What unlived life of my parents am I still carrying, and passing on to my descendants?* The parental voices of the past are very strong and according to Hollis it is often a common tendency for older adults to serve their message. The task of the second half of life is to find the natural source within and not be fearful of honoring one's own highly individual calling. Additionally, when the voices of past authority figures pose internal blockages for older adults, the result is often that these blockages are passed on to children in the form of emotional slavery, inability to take risks, and disaffirming attitudes towards sexuality, personal passions, and enthusiasms. Additionally, children then may become responsible for tending to their older parents' emotional needs.

3   *What, really, is my spirituality, and does it make me larger or smaller?* For many individuals, spirituality has become weighed down in religious dogma, guilt complexes, and agendas based on fear. Hollis's definition is that whatever "radically reframes the ego's sense of self and world, whatever obliges us to come in naked humility before the other anew is a spiritual encounter."[58] Spirituality takes many forms but when it is a mature spirituality that invites mystery it will produce a "quickening of the soul and body that is the spark of life."[59] Spirituality is what animates individuals and drives them forward. Cultivating this sense of mystery and numinous experience enlarges experience in the world and brings purpose and meaning to the older adult in the second half of life.

4   *Where do you refuse to grow up, wait for clarity before risking, hope of external solutions, expect rescue from someone, or wait for someone to tell you what your life is about?* Individuals have an inner

How We Age 27

frightened, isolated child who is looking for a caregiver. In order to finally grow up, adults beyond the middle years need to trust themselves instead of looking to partners, institutions, and ideologies for parenting. Although these sources may be helpful, ultimately growing up means discovering an individual truth. Older adults are ultimately responsible for their own journey and must challenge themselves to grow beyond their comfort zone in order to maintain a sense of meaning and purpose.

Gilda Frantz, a beloved Jungian elder in the classical tradition, wrote about her personal experience with the aging process.[60] She likened aging to a journey in which it is best to pack less rather than more. According to Frantz, for this trip into old age you must leave behind most "outer things" and only bring what is essential. Frantz's packing list for the journey into the last part of life includes one's imagination and dreams.

Another important element to aging well according to Frantz is that "we must each live our lives as though life is eternal, and quixotically we must be prepared for our death."[61] It is in this reconciliation of opposites that we can be spiritually alive. She explains that "paradoxically those who want to live well have to learn to die well."[62] Towards this end Frantz believes it is important to acquaint oneself with the inevitability of death.

Frantz also emphasized the need to be spiritually connected to something larger than our own being. She spoke about how easy it is to sink into life's tasks and lose spark and inner life. Frantz maintained that the spirit within us is made manifest by constant contact with it. Further, part of retrieving and safeguarding vitality and relatedness is allowing oneself to be honest with one's self and cultivate self-acceptance.

Johnson and Ruhl focused their attention on unlived potential in the second half of life.[63] As part of their treatment on the subject, they developed an *Unlived Life Inventory* as an exercise to help their readers discover qualities that have been lived, possibilities that have been cast off or closed, and potentials that the person would still like to fulfill. The total score for the inventory is based on the following four sub scores:[64]

1 *Outer life score.* Outer life is a dimension of external experiences and outer activity. It aims to determine how effectively and comfortably the participant is with the *doing* aspects of life.
2 *Inner life score.* Inner life is a dimension of subjective experiences of your personal self. It aims to determine how the participant feels about himself, his self-confidence, and his personal relationships with others.

28　*How We Age*

3　*Deeper life score.* Deeper life is a dimension of intuitive and creative experiences. It aims to determine how the participant relates to aspects of his experience that appear to be outside of his conscious control.
4　*Greater life score.* Greater life is a dimension of the higher Self or the transpersonal connection to the divine. It aims to determine how related the participant is to spirituality, core values, and aspirations.

Each of these four scores is a measure of realization and actualization of potential in that dimension. The total Whole Life Inventory score gives a measure of the development and satisfaction the participant is experiencing in his life at present. The inventory is designed to help the reader see where the person may be over or under-identified with certain aspects of being. The results also give the participant a picture of the areas of life that are more lived in contrast to areas that are relatively unlived. The authors advocate that the ultimate goal of wholeness in the second half of life can best be reached when there is a dynamic balance that enables a person to access all the possibilities of self.

In conclusion, Jungian psychology has offered the unique perspective that individuation, becoming oneself as fully as possible, is a lifetime enterprise that requires a continual reformulation of meaning, values, purposes, and activities.[65] As such, Jung envisioned the second half of life as a time of opportunity, in which growth and increasing degrees of wholeness and wisdom can emerge.[66] This orientation sees the life beyond the middle years as one with much promise for the individual and society as a whole.

This book looks to women's voices and lived experience, through interviews with women post-midlife, to examine and learn how individuals find meaning and purpose while navigating the aging process. While there are many theories and quantitative studies looking at this time in life, there are few qualitative studies that have explored the lived experience of older adults. The interviews presented here explored how older adults are being generative, seeking meaning, and individuating.

Notes

1　Baltes & Baltes, 1990; Reker, 2001; Rowe Kahn, 1997; Ryff, 1989; Schulz & Heckhausen, 1996.
2　Baltes & Baltes, 1990.
3　Reker, 2001.
4　Garfein & Herzog, 1995; Jorm et al., 1998; K. Morgan et al., 1991.
5　Reker, 2001, p. 45.
6　Adler, 1958; Frankl, 1985; James, 1902; Jung, 1971; Maslow, 1962; Rogers, 1980.
7　Erikson, 1963.

How We Age 29

8 Brown & Lowis, 2003.
9 Martens & Peedicayil, 2012.
10 Ibid.
11 Erikson, 1963.
12 Brown & Lowis, 2003.
13 Carlson, Seeman, & Fried, 2000; Glass et al., 2004; Schoklitsch & Baumann, 2012; Villar, 2012; Warburton, McLaughlin, & Pinsker, 2006.
14 Glass et al., 2004.
15 Ibid.
16 Warburton, McLaughlin, & Pinsker, 2006.
17 Schoklitsch & Baumann, 2012.
18 Frankl, 1985.
19 Crumbaugh & Maholick, 1969; Steger, Frazier, Oishi, & Kaler, 2006.
20 Ju et al., 2013; Krause, 2012; Martens, Goldenberg, & Greenberg, 2005.
21 Sinnott, 2009.
22 Ibid.
23 Malette & Oliver, 2006; Zanjiran et al., 2015.
24 Malette & Oliver, 2006; Zanjiran et al., 2015.
25 Ju et al., 2013; Krause, 2012; Martens et al., 2005.
26 Jung, 1960.
27 Sawin, 2014, p. 9.
28 Braam et al., 2006; Nakagawa, 2007; Scarcello, 2010; Tornstam, 1997, 2005, 2011; von Humboldt, Leal, & Pimenta, 2014.
29 Tornstam, 2005.
30 Tornstam, 2011.
31 Ibid.
32 Ibid.
33 Braam et al., 2006; Nakagawa, 2007; Scarcello, 2010; von Humboldt et al., 2014.
34 Library of Congress, 2012.
35 Corbett, 2014b, pp. 26–29.
36 Jung, 1960.
37 Mattoon, 2005.
38 Ibid.
39 Jung, 1989.
40 Ibid., p. 325.
41 Costello, 2014.
42 Ibid.
43 Costello, 2014, p. 168.
44 Corbett, 2014a.
45 Ruhl & Evans, 2014.
46 Ibid.
47 Ibid., p. 183.
48 Corbett, 2014b.
49 Ibid.
50 Hanna, 2014, pp. 126–127.
51 Hanna, 2014.
52 Costello, 2014.
53 Tennyson, 1860.
54 Hollis, 2005, 2014.

30 *How We Age*

55 Hollis, 2014, p. 207.
56 Ibid., p. 206.
57 Ibid., p. 207.
58 Ibid., pp. 209–210.
59 Ibid., p. 208.
60 Frantz, 2014.
61 Ibid., p. 162.
62 Ibid., p. 162.
63 Johnson & Ruhl, 2007.
64 Ibid., p. 244.
65 Cambray, 2014.
66 Jung, 1960.

3 Women's Voices and Lived Experience

Existential Pursuits and Affirmation of Life

The need for a new understanding of the post-midlife years emerges from both increasing lifespans and a realization of how living longer impacts both individuals and society. Towards the goal of furthering our understanding of later life, this author elected to go directly to women who are successfully navigating the post-midlife years and interview them regarding *how* they are making their lives meaningful. Utilizing a qualitative research method for analyzing social phenomenon (Interpretative Phenomenological Analysis or IPA) allowed me to explore the *process* by which women create meaningful and purposeful lives.[1] Qualitative approaches, in contrast to quantitative research, have the advantage of allowing in-depth and detailed study of experiences that are not easily quantifiable.[2] Also, the qualitative approach is uniquely designed to explore and understand the *meaning* individuals and groups assign to human experiences and social problems.[3] Additionally, qualitative inquiry uniquely honors efforts made at studying complex life experiences from a personal perspective.[4] Lastly, the IPA method encourages the researcher to engage with the participants' words and text in an interpretative fashion that allows the researcher access to an individual's cognitive inner world.[5] All of these elements made a qualitative approach, and IPA in particular, the perfect vehicle to study meaning-making in later life. (See Appendix A for more on methodology.)

The opportunity to listen to these women speak about their personal experiences with aging and meaning-making was a remarkable invitation to enter their private domain and learn from their experiences. The women I interviewed were between the ages of 63 and 73 years old. All the women had been married between 36 and 50 years, had adult children, and were grandparents. These women were experts on their own aging process and could provide a detailed understanding of their inner experience. In keeping with IPA methodology and coding, themes emerged through the data analysis. Table 3.1 presents a summary of the themes that emerged

Table 3.1 Meaning-Making in Later Life

Superordinate Themes	Subtheme 1	Subtheme 2	Subtheme 3	Subtheme 4
A Existential Pursuits	Capitalizing upon Self-Understanding	Considering Death	Fostering a Spiritual Connection	Leaving a Legacy/Sharing Wisdom
B Affirmation of Life	Engaging in Mentally Stimulating Activities	Engaging with Creativity	Engaging in Physical Activity	Engaging in Life-Long Learning
C Human Relationships	Connections with Family	Connections with Friends	Connections through Giving Back	Connections with Rekindled Relationships from the Past
D Resiliency	Medical Resilience	Psychological Resilience	Resilience to Life Circumstances	Resilience to a Changing World

and will be discussed. In the discussion that follows, quotes from the interviews will be shared in order to provide transparency and illustrate how the themes were expressed. All the participants' names have been altered however to preserve confidentiality.

Superordinate Theme A: Existential Pursuits

The results of this research showed that many women at this life stage are entertaining philosophical questions. Whereas marriage, children, and career may have held their attention in earlier years, these individuals have expanded their thinking to broader issues. Marion, an educator in her early seventies, shared:

> I was thinking about it before you came. I thought, you know, when you're younger—the worst decades in my life, I think, were supposed to be the best. My teen years, my twenties, even early thirties, were times of tremendous stress. I realize now it's because I was creating my life. I didn't know. I didn't know what would be. There was tremendous anxiety and need to define myself, and to prove myself, and to make these crucial life decisions. Everything depended on these crucial life decisions. Now, it's much better. Much, much better. Those decisions are in the past, they've been made, there's no changing it. How do you find meaning? At this point in your life, you see the arc of your life. You can tell the story of your life. Whereas, the early years, you're so busy writing it that you can't see it.

The thematic results showed that the physical and emotional time and space of later adulthood allows some individuals to turn their thoughts to other matters. For many of the participants in this study, a sense of freedom and exploration was emphasized—a sense that they suggested was impossible to navigate in their earlier years.

Subtheme 1: Capitalizing upon Self-Understanding

The participants highlighted that the process of growing older allows for maturity and self-reflection. The results showed that those who successfully create meaning in later adulthood are able to use this self-understanding as a launching pad to reach areas of potential that remained untapped or not fully realized in their earlier years. Of particular note was the idea that participants were no longer as concerned as they were in younger years about "keeping up appearances" and meeting others' expectations. This position was emphasized as affording them tremendous freedom to focus on activities that

34 *Existential Pursuits and Affirmation of Life*

they find nurturing and fulfilling. Sabina, a woman in her early sixties who works as a professional volunteer and part-time bookkeeper for the family business, explains that age has given her the opportunity to "pick and choose" how she will invest her time. Sabina said, "I feel I'm old enough to say 'no' if I want to.... I give myself the opportunity to say, 'I don't want to do that.'" Several participants voiced the same sentiments but often felt "selfish" in their decision to pursue activities that spoke to their hearts instead of fulfilling "societal obligations." This fear did not stop the participants from following their "calling" but still left them feeling a bit guilty. Bonnie, a retired doctor in her mid sixties who spent much of her adult life doing long hospital shifts, reported feeling "sort of bad, like what am I doing here on a Wednesday afternoon doing pottery instead of surgery?" She stated that she felt more reassured after speaking to a male friend from another medical field, who explained that the first 30 years are formative years for education, getting married, and building a family. The second 30 years are to work very hard. Then, he said, "The third 30 years is when you enjoy yourself." Bonnie added, "He sees a lot of old people so he's always been very good about seeing the span of life." Marion also spoke about this idea of "selfishness" but explained that her friends are trying to help her expand her image of herself:

> I, as a person, have become more sure of myself, more competent, more self-motivated. I'm not as concerned about what people think about me. I don't care what the community thinks, what the neighbors think. I want to do what I want to do. Much more selfish. I feel selfish. My women's group met yesterday and we talked about this. They said, "That's not selfishness. That's self-awareness and self-actualization. That's not selfishness." I said, "It feels a little selfish to me."

The results of this study suggested that the participants are concerned with nurturing others and continue to measure themselves by external standards. Nonetheless, finding meaning in later life seems to entail coming to terms with these issues. Ella, an educator in her late sixties, also discussed this tension:

> I'm trying to be a little more, what I would say, selfish, but that's not … it would be selfless, I guess. I used to feel invisible and everybody else's needs were more important than mine, so that's a definite shift that my needs are as important as anybody else's in the room, and learning how to ask for the help that I need or the ear, or the heart, or the soul of someone else. That's been a shift and that's something I'm moving towards more.

The voices and lived experiences of these women echo Jung's ideas about the individuation process in later life—a time in which people continue to develop and mature throughout the lifespan.[6] In particular these women's concerns about listening to and developing their authentic selves was very much in keeping with the words of the Jungian analyst, James Hollis.[7] Hollis described the "second half of life" as a time of caring less about "keeping up appearances" and meeting others' expectations. He explained that much of earlier adulthood can be viewed as a process of adaptation and adjustment to others' expectations as a means to efficiently raise family, develop careers, and generally to make one's place in the world. In contrast, Hollis maintained that the second half of life is a time to develop one's authentic self: a time to soften the voices of authority figures and listen instead to the more personal voice of the soul. Hollis's ideas about finding one's authentic self mirror the finding in this study that older adults tend to shrug off societal and community expectations. The subtheme of capitalizing upon self-understanding is consistent with Jung and his current followers' thoughts that self-understanding is an essential quality that undergirds the capacity to individuate and thereby lead a meaningful life in later adulthood.

Subtheme 2: Considering Death

All of the participants spoke about their mortality and how it affects them. Most of the women interviewed did not fear their own demise, but rather viewed death as both a given and a motivator to grab life in the moment. The data showed that it is this orientation that perhaps helps them see each day as an opportunity rather than a step closer to the grave.

Marion's response to the question of whether she fears her own death was, "No, my husband's 76. I'm 73. We could die tomorrow. I'm not afraid of his dying. I'm not afraid of my dying." Marion does speak, however, about the idea of death serving as a motivator. She says, "It makes me anxious to get done what I want to get done ... because there's a deadline. You've got a deadline. You get energized right before your deadline, right?"

Bonnie explained how the idea of death motivated her to retire early from her demanding job as a physician so that she could enjoy all that life has to offer:

Both my parents died at age 72. My father died of colon cancer at 72 before they did colonoscopies. Like 30 years ago. He never smoked, always exercised, was in really good shape. My mother who smoked and probably drank and who knows what else she did, died at 72 of

36   *Existential Pursuits and Affirmation of Life*

pancreatic cancer. When the option came to retire early that really was in the back of my mind.... Life can be short.

Participants also expressed a sense of gratitude for the lives that they have had so far and an understanding that life is time-limited. Rose, a retired educator and professional volunteer in her early seventies, voiced her feelings: "I feel like I've had a really rich, full life.... I'm certainly not ready to die, I don't want to die. If something were to happen though I wouldn't feel like I've been robbed." Sabina spoke about appreciating life and hoping it will not end too soon:

> I want to appreciate my life. I want to appreciate that I'm here. I lost a mother when she was 60. I lost two very close girlfriends to cancer at very young ages. As we all have ... I want to try to do what I can to have as much time as I can.... I know that that conveyor belt is on and I know that day-by-day we still continue to move toward whatever the end will be. I just really right now don't want it to be so soon. I seem to have so much to be thankful for.... I know that things happen. We always say live every day like it's your last day. I'm not sure that I live every day like it's my last day. I'd like to say that I do or try to but I don't know that that's realistic. I do appreciate getting up in the morning.

Another participant, Ella, whose own mother died in her early forties, said she used to have a fear of dying at a young age. Now, she says, she has come to terms with the impermanence of life. Ella shares her philosophy that, "all of our days are numbered. I understand that now. So, it's what you make of the time that you have." Further, Ella expresses her gratitude each night when she goes to bed by saying: "Thank you, God, for another day and if tomorrow is my last, I'm a very content, happy person."

Women post-midlife who are successfully making meaning in their lives have entertained ideas about their death and have used their gratitude and existential awareness as a foundation upon which to build their current lives. These results are consistent with the literature reviewed previously. The Jungian perspective, as articulated by Costello, explained that fleeing the laws of nature (e.g., death) can create further suffering.[8] Additionally, the terror management theory postulated that concerns about death enhance the need to view the world as a meaningful place.[9] Frantz's reflections also supported these findings: Writing as a Jungian in later adulthood, she offered a reminder that those who want to live well have to learn to accept death.[10] The findings of this study in conjunction with the literature strongly suggest that life's meaning is renewed by looking mortality squarely in the eye. This vantage point points to a strong connection between the need to become acquainted with death and reaping meaning in later life.

Subtheme 3: Fostering a Spiritual Connection

The results around spirituality revealed three different groupings: (a) Those who are religiously connected; (b) those who see their life activities infused with spirituality; and (c) those who are envious of others who are spiritually or religiously connected. Although only some of the participants were involved in organized religion, several other women represented their lives and daily activities in spiritual terms. It appeared that these women had infused spirituality into their everyday endeavors and thereby elevated the personal significance and numinous quality of their activities.

Ella is representative of the first group, those who are religiously connected. She became more religious as a consequence of her son becoming a religious leader. Although first put off that her son changed course from the manner in which he was raised, she now admits that her son and his family have had a profound effect on her spiritually and religiously. Ella says that she used to live in fear of death, due to her mother's early death, but has evolved. She says that her "friends now know that it's not that I'm fearless, but I live in faith not fear, and that's a favorite expression of mine."

Marion has also suffused her activities with spirituality. When she speaks about her pottery, the listener feels transported to another realm as the activity of making pots is elevated to a higher dimension:

> The process consists of the four ancient elements: earth, air, water, and fire. That's how pottery is made. I like the primitive, basic, natural quality of it.... I don't do pretty little things. The glazing is my specialty, really.... The glazing is what I find most—and the shape. The shape and the glazing, yeah, I just find it sensual, with your hands in clay. Sensual. The process of working on a wheel is centering. You're centering the clay, but the whole process centers oneself. It's calming and meditative, at the same time that it's very exciting and demanding. Like music, like playing an instrument, you've never reached perfection no matter how long or hard you work on it. You never get to the end point, so you never get bored. It's always challenging.

Along with Sabina, Heidi, a woman in her late sixties who is the CEO/ Founder of an organization that helps individuals with special needs, falls into the category of wishing she had a spiritual connection. Heidi shared:

38   *Existential Pursuits and Affirmation of Life*

"I envy people who really believe there's a God. I really do and the older I get the less I believe." Sabina feels that she is struggling to find a spiritual path but has not found an outlet that currently works for her: "I think it brings peace. I think there are certain things that bring peace. I think that's really a big deal because it can only make things clearer and better and not so mixed up and tainted."

While the subtheme of fostering a spiritual connection is expressed differently for all the participants, it seems to be an element that plays an important role in meaning-making in later life. The ability to step away from the mundane and look at a picture larger than one's own existence is one that is either realized or that generates struggle for many at this stage of life.

Subtheme 4: Leaving a Legacy/Sharing Wisdom

Several participants during the course of the interview spoke about the meaning cultivated through leaving a legacy. From their descriptions, it seemed that "legacy" could take many forms. For these participants, there was an experience of leaving something precious behind in their name, whether it be a business, an influential relationship, or creating opportunities for others through community work. Sabina, for example, expressed the idea of leaving a legacy from two different sources: (a) Building a family business that spans four generations, starting with her grandfather, and (b) community work that helps spring young adults into adulthood through college and religious education. Other participants spoke about the legacy they hope to leave by mentoring younger professionals. Marion described her personal relationship with a younger teacher:

> The one place where I see meaning-making is when I'm mentoring student teachers and I feel, "This is very meaningful. This is passing on the mantle." There's one teacher who was my student three or four years ago. She's become my kind of intellectual daughter. I meet with her, and I adore her, and she likes me. I'm passing on thinking, or this book, or this article. It's more a friendship now, because she's rising up in the academic world.

Heidi and Ella spoke about the legacy they hope to leave with their children and grandchildren. Heidi said, "Our legacy is the people we leave behind, who remember us." Ella felt that she missed inheriting so much from her own mother and yearns to leave an impression with her children and grandchildren. Ella says legacy is linked to the following:

I now have a relationship, or multiple relationships with my grand-children where they really know who I am. I know any one of them could speak at my funeral and I would be proud of them representing me. I have that perspective because I was nine when my mom died. Much of who I became and what interests me was being the mother that I never received for generations of children, both as a classroom teacher and then as an administrator. Now, I've just narrowed that frame. It's most important to me that my children and grandchildren know who I am, as opposed to the children of strangers.

Meaning-making in later adulthood appears to be associated with leaving something of oneself behind in this world and making a difference through one's own actions. The expression of this subtheme takes on many forms but is constant as a strong undercurrent in peoples' narratives.

As a variant on the above theme, the data showed that another source of meaning-making for participants post-midlife was sharing wisdom that they have accrued through their personal lives. Both Ella and Marion plan to write books to pass on what they have learned. Ella revealed that she has personally grown, adjusted, and now flourished through her adult son's choice to become a dedicated religious leader so that now she can impart wisdom about adjusting to adult children's choices. She says: "One of the goals that I had when I retired was to write a book, a book based on when your adult children don't turn out the way you expected them to." She points to adult children's choices of partners, sexual preferences, and religious affiliations as some of the thorny issues that often interfere in parent-child relationships. She has worked out some of these challenges in her own relationship with her son and wants to share her wisdom. Through her personal life, she now sees how parents and adult children can impact each other positively, once certain obstacles are traversed.

Marion wrote a book about 10 years ago (when she was in her early sixties), which was the story of raising her child, who was a creative child prodigy. She explains, "It's a very challenging story of a non-musician parent in possession of a child who is a musician. Maybe it's an advice book for parents who are finding themselves in a similar situation." Marion's advice is universal in that many children "fall far from the tree" and she uses her own story to describe the flexibility required to raise a child who does not conform to mainstream expectations at school, home, or society at large. She is also in the process of writing another book, primarily for her kids, which will be a collection of things she has learned in life. One of the first recommendations, aimed at not getting mired in the logistics and details of life, would be not to get bogged down with cooking as you can "always order in." Meaning-making post-midlife seems to

40　*Existential Pursuits and Affirmation of Life*

include leaving a legacy and sharing wisdom with the next generation. The process of taking ownership of one's accumulated knowledge and accomplishments and passing these treasures to others is a signal to oneself and others that life has been well lived thus far.

The study's finding that meaning-making in later life is connected to leaving a legacy is consistent with the literature. Erikson's seventh developmental stage of Generativity versus Stagnation emphasized the impetus to nurture, guide, and ensure the well-being of future generations and leave a lasting legacy.[11] Current theorists and researchers have also proposed that generativity plays a significant role in the final decades of life.[12] Villar drew upon Erikson's later writings when he adopted the term of grand generativity to explain the helping and supportive activities of older people.[13]

The finding that sharing wisdom is an important variable in meaning-making for older adults is also found in the literature. According to Sinnott, Viktor Frankl emphasized that it is essential for wisdom rather than biological or genetic factors to be the primary focus of aging in order to avoid a crisis of meaning in old age.[14] Frankl maintained that aging adults must be lifted and re-humanized to enable them to see themselves as larger than their losses. Moreover, wisdom can play an important part in this transforming sense of self. Corbett also addressed the topic of wisdom in two of his developmental tasks.[15] In maintenance of self-esteem, Corbett emphasized the need for older adults to value their knowledge and wisdom. In the developmental task of taking on new roles and responsibilities, Corbett stressed the need for older adults to share their wisdom with family and share their fund of knowledge, maturity, and experience through engagement in civic roles. The idea that sharing wisdom is an important part of meaning-making in later adulthood can thus be found both in this study's findings and in the contributions of existential-humanistic and Jungian scholars.

Summary: Existential Pursuits

The themes reflected in the participant narratives pointed to later adulthood as a time of existential pondering and soul-searching. In particular, participants were self-reflective and motivated to use this self-understanding to better their current lives. Also, the results pointed to women who were facing their mortality and using the idea of a defined lifespan to propel themselves forward to live life to its fullest. Further, spirituality, leaving a legacy, and sharing wisdom were recurring themes in the data that were entwined with finding meaning post-midlife.

Superordinate Theme B: Affirmation of Life

The thematic results of this research showed that many women in later life look to life-affirming activities and attitudes that engage their intellect, creativity, bodies, and souls. These activities bring a sense of fulfillment and purpose in addition to providing opportunities to explore areas previously uncharted. Many of the participants sounded like children who were finally able to enter the candy shop. Their excitement had a contagious quality. Marion explains: "I finally have time to go into some of my interests. I didn't have this time when I was raising kids (and working). I was too busy with their interests." The data also highlighted that there was a tension between enjoying unstructured time and gravitating towards scheduling appealing activities that coalesced into a weekly routine.

Subtheme 1: Engaging in Mentally Stimulating Activities

The results indicated that the participants were drawn to a variety of intellectually stimulating activities that they deemed meaningful. While individual interest varied, the participants were all involved with some sort of enrichment. Some participants still derived excitement from work. Heidi, for example, is still fully involved in the company she founded. She speaks with pride and positive energy when describing her company and the meaning it holds for her: "It's about 280 people and we provide all sorts of services: child development services, speech therapy, educational therapy, occupational therapy, and our biggest program is actually behavioral intervention for autistic individuals." Heidi adds:

> I like the challenge of the job. It's the challenge of starting a new program and putting it together. Hiring people, seeing it go in, learning how to document what you do. How to bill it, how to justify it, how to work with insurance companies, how to work with school districts, rules, regulations. How do you do a good job within the constraints of what you're given? Yeah, it's a huge challenge.

When speaking about what energizes her in life today, she says, "Seeing clients do well, seeing improvements, seeing my staff be excited by what they've succeeded in doing energizes me." Other participants have more leisure time due to cutting back to part-time work or being fully retired. These individuals have pursued interests that have taken them in many different directions. Rose speaks with great excitement about her volunteer work with an organization that helps nonprofits through coaching, consulting, and capacity-building. She describes her current assignment with enthusiasm:

42   *Existential Pursuits and Affirmation of Life*

Now I'm on a project that has been a really great project. There's a four-person team. We're working in East Los Angeles with a school. We just did a big analysis of the school and we're going to help them through a strategic plan. This is the first time they've assigned me to anything that was school-related.... This one is really good, but the reason I like it, really like it, is because most of the other ones they put me on I was alone. It was kind of one-on-one coaching for a new Executive Director that kind of thing. This one, there's a team of four of us. So it's much more stimulating, it's much more comprehensive stuff. I would say, in March, I spent probably eight or ten hours a week on the project. We just did a big presentation on Monday, now we're going into the next phase.

Sabina is involved in a dog-rescue organization and various community organizations that support religious education, college education, and summer camping for children. She described the excitement and challenge she now feels with fundraising based on what she absorbed as a young woman still learning the ropes. The story she tells is based on a younger version of herself nervously soliciting an older gentleman for money. The phone solicitation started with some small talk with the gentleman and then the conversation became more pointed:

Then he said, "What do you want?" Just like that. I remember it as clear as day and I said, I was stumbling, I said, "I want to ask you for money." He says, "Then just ask me. Just ask." Just pure and simple. Then he said something and I always carry it with me. He said, "If you hadn't asked me … if you ask somebody for something; one, the worst thing you're going to hear is "no." If that's the worst thing you're going to hear then you really need to get a tougher skin." Two, I was giving him … this is what he said, I was giving him the opportunity to participate in something that he would not have had the opportunity to participate in if I hadn't called him. It stayed with me. No matter if I'm asking for $250, $250,000, at this point in my life it's almost as though if I hear "no," I hear "no." Maybe I didn't present it properly. Maybe I didn't present it where it was passionate or the passion wasn't there for that person. It's also giving these people and … it's giving the opportunity for people to participate in something. It could be a dinner, it could be an event, it could be anything.... I think everybody wants to feel wanted. Everybody wants to feel as though they're participating in something or they're doing something of value. I find that of value. And the older I've gotten the more important it seems to be to me.

Existential Pursuits and Affirmation of Life 43

Participants also spoke about the stimulation involved in traveling, book groups, taking classes, and learning new skills. Rose described her book club group that is in its ninth year: "We all love literature, we love learning and we love getting together. It's a very serious book group. They're pretty much all major travelers. We read fiction, we read non-fiction, we read books from all over the world." She also shared how she has redirected the passion she felt towards science as a science teacher into "our travels, our collections, our garden, everything is kind of science. I'm enjoying it now with my grandchildren, so that's kind of good."

The data showed that using their intellect in one manner or another nourished the participants. These results suggest that activities that stimulate cognitive processes are involved with creating a meaningful life in later adulthood. The literature similarly points to the benefit of learning and growing in relation to creating and maintaining meaning in later life. Frantz shared about her own aging process viewed within a Jungian lens.[16] She describes the need to stay mentally flexible and adaptive in order to age well. Towards this goal, she prescribed actively searching for new knowledge as a means to stimulate the brain. Corbett, Johnston and Ruhl, and Hollis also focused on the importance of attending to and developing unlived potential in the second half of life.[17] This type of exploration requires a person to attend to one's curiosity and passion in a way that is often mentally stimulating. The study's findings, in combination with the literature, point to the importance of engaging in meaningful learning endeavors as a means to create meaning post-midlife.

Subtheme 2: Engaging with Creativity

Most of the participants in the study were engaged with creative activity that they equated with meaning-making. They spoke about these creative pursuits with great passion and excitement. Marion, for example described taking up piano in her early seventies:

> What I'm most excited about, right now, like the last month of my life, is I decided to play an instrument.... I had a piano tuner over two weeks ago Tuesday. I had the piano tuned, and the next day had my first lesson.... I am thrilled. In the hour before you came, I practiced. I'm probably practicing two hours a day. I am loving it.

Half of the participants spoke about their work with pottery. Bonnie, a retired surgeon, shared that pottery is "like surgery with no risk." Rose, in speaking about pottery, explains:

44 *Existential Pursuits and Affirmation of Life*

> I am very much enjoying my forays into the arts. That's something I never had time for.... I am currently taking pottery classes and having a great time with that.... I'm having a good time especially because I can make pots to put my plants in.... I like working with my hands a lot.

Marion calls herself a serious potter and works in the studio approximately three hours per day. She is always looking for a challenge and a new area to learn. In speaking about glazes for her pottery she says, "I am always learning something new. I exhausted the glazes at my studio so I found a whole new company that makes all these glazes. They're so gorgeous. Now, I'm working with a new kind of glazing."

Other participants looked to different creative endeavors. Ella, for example, realized that when she fully retires she has an interest in returning to singing and acting, a serious hobby that she pursued in high school. Although her current schedule is full with part-time work and being a hands-on grandmother, she explains:

> I think I've always wanted singing lessons and I've always wanted to be part of an ensemble and so there are theater groups out there and I know of people that would give me singing lessons. I want to start that before I retire, so it's already in place.

Several participants spoke about writing projects and the process of creation itself. The data suggest that the creative process is intimately connected to meaning-making in later adulthood. The process of creating seems to change focus and evolve over the lifespan from creating careers and families in the earlier years to creative expression through artistic pursuits in later adulthood.

The literature also pointed to the power of creativity in older adults' lives. Corbett amplified Jung's suggestions regarding creativity in older adulthood by drawing on the idea that the person who does not build will demolish and destroy.[18] In other words, creativity is essential in older adults' lives as a path to both prevent emotional decline and to maintain psychological well-being and aliveness. Hanna similarly described creativity as a vehicle that contributes to the older adult's self-esteem and capacity to feel engaged in life.[19] She suggested three entry points to the engagement in creative expression or activities for older adults: the beginning participant, the returning participant and the life-long participant. Regardless at what point the older adult enters this creative world, artistic expression can bring joy, comfort, and a renewed sense of meaning and purpose. The findings of this study similarly make a strong case that creativity is an important medium for meaning-making in later life.

Existential Pursuits and Affirmation of Life 45

Subtheme 3: Engaging in Physical Activity

The data showed that many participants are engaged in physical activity. For some participants, exercising is a direct form of meaning-making and for others exercising is a means to help ensure the possibility of retaining a quality life that holds meaning. The idea of movement combined with nature seems to be a particularly potent combination for some participants. Rose speaks about hiking, biking, and gardening with her husband and friends. At one point in the conversation, she looked at this researcher in embarrassment to ask, "Am I too happy?" In describing her work with succulents, she said:

> It takes about one second for my husband and I to be talked into going into the yard and puttering out in the yard, re-potting or finding … it's not a chore for us, usually. So those things are all good.

Bonnie shared that she enjoys hiking, Pilates, and yoga on a weekly basis. She explained that this physical activity is both enjoyable and helps alleviate the back pain she developed while working as a surgeon:

> I have a Pilates teacher I love.… I walk with the neighbors.… I do yoga at the gym. If I go my neck and back are fine. When I miss a couple of weeks something gets screwed up.… Doctors screw up their backs and necks. Every single person that retired from our department has had a bad neck or back.

Ella experienced a debilitating bacterial infection two years ago and as a result now tries to do some physical activity for 30 minutes almost every day. Ella shared that she enjoys exercising by herself as she is more comfortable not going to a gym and "feeling judged." Ella explains, "I work out with a trainer, and it's one-on-one, or I walk or hike or do whatever, mostly but myself." Physical activity was a part of most of the participants' lives. In some instances, movement and being outdoors were fulfilling and energizing activities for their own sake. For others, physical activity was more of an insurance plan to allow them to continue to have quality lives filled with meaning and purpose.

Subtheme 4: Engaging in Life-Long Learning

The data showed that the participants were drawn to learning new things throughout the lifespan. The idea of growth through learning was evidenced in many of the narratives. Marion, who is an educator, says, "I'm

46 *Existential Pursuits and Affirmation of Life*

not a teacher at my core, I'm a learner." Further she explains, "I'm always looking for new things. I think one thing that keeps me going, is that there's so much to learn. There's so much out there. There's so many interesting things in the world. I am very curious, to a fault." Marion's attraction to learning is evident when she shares, "I'd like to study geology and I'd like to study astronomy. I don't know much about astronomy. I know probably more than most people, but I'd like to learn more about physics and astronomy."

Ella, who mentors student teachers, spoke of life-long learning in terms of the ever-continuing journey involved in self-reflection. She sees the search for self-knowledge as a fuel that can energize one towards personal growth and expansion. Ella shares this idea:

> I've always been reflective. It's a teaching stance. We teach our students that reflection is one of the most important gifts you can give yourself as a teacher, so that you go into a lesson and you teach it and then you sit and you say, "What went well? What didn't? How can I redo it? How can I grow?" I guess I've always come from that perspective. It's always about growth and life-long learning, which is a catch phrase for a lot, but I think learning about yourself, learning about your place in the universe and what your gifts are, that's one of those things I've always shared with my students and my children.

The findings suggest that older adults engaged in life-long learning experience their lives to be enriched with energy and vitality. Retaining and continually developing a curiosity about the world and a thirst for knowledge both energizes and propels the post-midlife adult to feel more fully involved in life. Within the literature, Hollis also spoke about how meaning in the second half of life is dependent upon addressing psychological obstacles that might interfere with enlarged thinking and sparking of curiosity.[20] He suggested that older adults may need to ask themselves how they have let go of their goals due to fear, not "showing up," or harsh internal voices that negate their individual calling. He suggested that this honest soul-searching often results in recovering an interest, talent, or enthusiasm for life being relinquished. Hollis also explained that part of meaning-making post-midlife may require one to challenge oneself beyond his or her comfort zone.

Summary: Affirmation of Life

The themes reflected in participant narratives pointed to a connection between meaning-making post-midlife and an engagement in life-affirming

Existential Pursuits and Affirmation of Life   47

activities and attitudes. This engagement in life was seen through intellectual, creative, and physical endeavors. It also was a "learning stance" attitude towards the self that can propel individuals towards greater growth and expansion.

Notes

1 Barker, Pistrang, & Elliot, 2003; Creswell, 2014; French, Maissi, & Marteau, 2005; Maxwell, 2005.
2 Barker, Pistrang, & Elliott, 2003; Creswell, 1998, 2014; Henwood & Pidgeon, 1992; Maxwell, 2005; Smith, 1996a, 1996b; Turpin et al., 1997.
3 Creswell, 2014.
4 Ibid.
5 Biggerstaff & Thompson, 2008.
6 Jung, 1960.
7 Hollis, 2014.
8 Costello, 2014.
9 Martens et al., 2005.
10 Frantz, 2014.
11 Erikson, 1963.
12 Carlson, Seeman, & Fried, 2000; Glass et al., 2004; Schoklitsch & Baumann, 2012; Villar, 2012; Warburton, McLaughlin, & Pinsker, 2006.
13 Villar, 2012.
14 Sinnott, 2009; Frankl, 1985.
15 Corbett, 2014b.
16 Frantz, 2014.
17 Corbett, 2014b; Johnston & Ruhl, 2007; Hollis, 2005, 2014.
18 Corbett, 2014b.
19 Hanna, 2014.
20 Hollis, 2014.

4 Women's Voices and Lived Experience

Human Relationships and Resiliency

While existential pursuits and affirmation of life were powerful themes within my participants' narratives, there were two other significant themes that emerged through the data: human relationships and resiliency. In order to be transparent and most effectively share these women's lived experience, I will use their voices once again through excerpts from their transcripts.

Superordinate Theme C: Human Relationships

The results of this study showed that human relationships were essential to finding meaning in later life. These human connections were seen in various intersecting circles of family, friends, community, and past childhood connections.

Subtheme 1: Connections with Family

The data showed that connections with family constitute an important element in bringing a sense of meaning to later life. All the participants spoke about their husbands, children, and extended family as being a major contributor to their sense of purpose, contentment, and well-being. Grandchildren, however, seem to be in their own special category as they carry enormous personal meaning for adults in later life. All of the participants repeatedly mentioned how gratified they are in their grandparent role. Some mentioned that they heard this rumor about the joys of grandparenthood from others, before becoming grandparents, but were nonetheless shocked by their own personal reactions. Marion shares that her grandchildren are the "best thing that ever happened to me in my whole life." She describes her first glimpse at this powerful emotion:

> Well, when you're a child, a young girl typically, you think about what it might be like to be married, what it would be like to be a wife,

Human Relationships and Resiliency 49

what it would be like to be a mother. You never fantasize about what it would be like to be a grandmother. I never had any expectations. I never had any idea what being a grandmother meant. I was blown away. When my first grandchild was born, I wasn't in the room. It was a difficult birth and there was a problem and they had a whole staff in there of nurses and pediatricians, the doctor. When she actually gave birth, they had to take the child immediately. Anyway, I wasn't there the moment of birth, but like 20 minutes later they said I could come in. My husband and I could come in. The door was open just this much, and I looked in first before I opened the door. There, on this, I guess it was a scale, bassinet, was this quivering mass of pink protoplasm. I felt like I'd been struck by Cupid's arrow. Something went through me that I had never experienced in my life. People say it's like falling in love, but I never had that lightning bolt of falling in love experience, but I had it when my first child was born and then again when my first grandchild was born. I fell in love with that little thing. Never gone away and now I have four of them.

Ella explained how she threw herself into her career when her own children were young and felt that she missed out on some of their childhood. She shares the following about her experience as a grandmother:

My grandchildren tapped something in me. Everyone says that grandchildren are the prize at the end of parenthood, it's really true. I said to myself, I've spent my entire career giving to other people's children and maybe didn't give as much to my own children as I had wished that I had the time to do, or the desire, if I'm being quite honest. It wasn't enough for me ever to just be a mom, but I began to feel differently once I had grandchildren. In 2009, my son had four children at that time and they relocated to LA and I decided I couldn't keep such a demanding job. I wouldn't have time to bring them into my world, so I retired (at that time) and had two fantastic years of being the grandmother I always hoped to be.

Rose shared how her relationships with her grandchildren have been particularly close and how these relationships have given her experiences that were not possible with her own children. She explains:

The two older ones lived with us for almost a year twice. We're very hands on, but we're really close to them and we take them on trips. It's much more satisfying than our own children, because I have always been really interested in science. My own children didn't

50 *Human Relationships and Resiliency*

really like science. Our grandchildren are nature buffs. They all collect things and want to go on trips. The 8-year-old knows everything there is to know about cats, wild cats, and is waiting for us to take her to Madagascar.

It appears from the data that family, and grandchildren in particular, play a very special role in bringing a sense of purpose and continuity to those in later life. All of the participants highlighted family and grandchildren as an extremely significant factor that contributes to their overall quality of life. In the literature, Ruhl and Evans also argued that humans need a supportive environment in order to achieve spiritual growth, meaning, and purpose.[1] The environment that supports this developmental state may be created within the powerful container of intimate and transformative relationships. Corbett specifically addressed ways in which the older adult must allow for mature dependence on adult children.[2] The role of grandparent can become developmentally important for elders, adult children, and grandchildren. The findings of this research similarly point to a strong relationship between finding meaning in the second half of life and connections with family.

Subtheme 2: Connections with Friends

The thematic results pointed to friends being another significant contributor to making a meaningful life post-midlife. Most of the participants are looking for different qualities in their new friends than the friends they chose when they were younger. While most of the participants have continued to associate with their long-time friends, their needs and interests have changed over the years and influenced their choices of new friends. Rose shared that she has made many new friends through her new interests and activities:

Now that we are retired we have lots of new friends…. We have tons of friends who are in our succulent group. We have friends that we exercise and bike with. Through our shared interests we've definitely made new friends. Through the Executive Service Corp., those are good friends … we all like each other … they are really, really nice people. Different, not educators, they were hospital administrators, or lawyers or accountants. It was like, "Wow these are interesting people."

Ella believes that she has changed some of her patterns in the type of person she picks as a friend. In the past, she was always the one doing

Human Relationships and Resiliency 51

most of the giving and she gravitated towards needier people. In later adulthood, she has tried to find friends who can reciprocate more. She describes the change:

> I've always been the listener. I've always been the supporter. I've always been the therapist without the license. I've always been the mentor without the degree. Whatever it is, that's who I am. In my retirement years however, I have been able to cultivate a couple of newer friends who are like me. There's great reciprocity. If I go for a hike with this one friend in particular, she was a school counselor, so she has the same skills. We have talked about how similar we are and that when we first start the hike it's, "Who's going to ask the first question?" but I don't have to worry, so if she says to me, "How are you?" before I get to say, "How are you?" I know there's going to be equal time for both of us to be open and share.

Further, many of the participants spoke about needing a counter-balance to their relationships with the husbands to whom they have been married for so many decades (36–50 years). The participants often felt that their emotional needs have changed over the years and their new girlfriends can fill in the gaps that their husbands cannot fill. Sabina described these relationships with other women:

> They're confidantes. I think women need women more than men need men. That's the way I see things. I think women cleave to women for certain emotional issues. There are certain things that you can get from your spouse…. I can talk to my husband about anything. But, there's some feedback and something that I get from speaking to my girlfriends. There's a commonality of our gender obviously and our experiences and things that are more enriching for me sometimes to speak to my girlfriend about an issue, if you will, than to speak to my husband.

Ella says that her husband, like her older friends, tends to be more centered around himself. She says when she was ill with her serious bacterial infection, she became more needy and yearned for a husband who could be a better caretaker. Today she says that her husband is trying to adjust but that she also is turning more towards her women friends:

> God willing, we'll both [Ella and her husband] live to be in our 90s and that will be it, but it's learning to make this relationship more than what it's been in terms of that reciprocity…. The illness triggered all of those feelings of, what do I need out of this relationship? How do

52   *Human Relationships and Resiliency*

> I remain true to what I need? Part of that is, I have cultivated girl-friends, which they say, at the end, we're all going to be these women in retirement homes anyway, that we have to have our sisters with us.

The data showed that relationships with friends are a significant factor in feeling that one's life has purpose and meaning. Further, it appears that people in later life are choosing different types of friends than the ones that they chose when they were younger. Additionally, while all the participants plan to remain married to their long-time spouses, they look for friends who fill in the gaps that their spouses are unable to fill.

Corbett's suggestions may shed some light on this need for different types of friends in later life.[3] He discussed the tasks of strengthening inferior functions and integrating contrasexual aspects of the personality as part of the individuation process in later adulthood. It appears that individuals may choose to have experiences with different types of people post-midlife as means of strengthening and developing different parts of the self to achieve wholeness. The results of this study indicate that the best way to strengthen undeveloped aspects of one's self may include an effort to associate and mingle with people who perceive and engage in the world differently from one's accustomed manner.

Another aspect of making friends that differ from those chosen in early adulthood might be linked to Hollis's idea that the second half of life is one that is concerned with developing one's authentic self.[4] Choosing friends based on how they fit in with one's family configuration (e.g., friends who have children of the same age and/or spouses that interact well with each other) or career situation (e.g., befriending people who may be integral in one's work life) may no longer be the important aspects involved in finding true friendship. In keeping with finding one's authentic self, Hollis emphasized this time in life as a time to risk change in order to serve "life, not death, growth not aversive adaptation" (p. 207). Related to these ideas, the findings showed that while individuals may be interested in making different types of friends, they may not want to destroy their long-time marriages nor most of their long-time friendships. Older adults appear to value the history and current companionship with their spouses but often acknowledged how they are different people than when they married their spouses in their twenties. Making different types of friends seems to help fill the gaps for older women.

Subtheme 3: Connections through Giving Back

The results of this study showed that the human relationships established in the process of giving back to others was a sustaining and enhancing

Human Relationships and Resiliency 53

element in the lives of older adults. The human contact involved in either helping individuals directly or organizationally allowed for a sense of intimacy and community. Ella discovered that she "was absolutely happier when I'm doing for someone else than I am for myself." She elaborated:

> I would just say that for me, learning that I'm happiest if ... it doesn't have to be big giving; it could just be being a sympathetic listener to a friend.... At the end of the day, I get into bed and I say to myself, "Well, what did I accomplish today?" If it was a day I saw my grand-kids, I would say, "Yes." If it were a day I had a meeting at an organization, I would say that was "good." If it was a day where I got up and walked the track at the park and had lunch with a friend, for me, that wasn't good enough.

Ella also mentioned that during a two-year stint at full retirement, she became ill. She described her thoughts: "At that time, I was happily retired and I had just recently been diagnosed and had made this plea bargain with God, Get me better, I'll give back."

Rose speaks about the sense of community that she experiences with fellow volunteers with whom she works at an organization that helps non-profits through coaching, consulting, and capacity-building: "They were all leaders in their fields. They're all quite accomplished. They're all educated; they're all passionate about their work.... Everybody shares certain values." Rose points to a phenomenon in which being with like-minded people who are working together towards a common goal builds a very satisfying community experience.

Marion speaks about the sense of fulfillment she receives when mentoring student teachers: "I get tremendous pleasure out of seeing them get it. Different areas of getting it, but they get it. They're so appreciative. They say, 'Thank you.' They write me the most beautiful notes."

The human relationships that are built in the course of giving back to others have multiple layers. One is the micro level in which a direct relationship is developed and enjoyed between the person giving and the person receiving. The second is the macro level in which a communal relationship develops around shared goals and values that are expressed through an organization. Adults in later life seem to derive meaning from both the relationships developed through direct giving and the community relationships that are built around organizational giving.

This finding, regarding the importance of relationships made through giving back, is related to two subjects in the literature that are usually discussed independently of each other: (a) Erikson's developmental stage of Generativity versus Stagnation; and (b) the importance of human

54   *Human Relationships and Resiliency*

relationships in later adulthood, as described by Ruhl and Evans, and Corbett.[5] In the process of enacting Erikson's seventh stage—nurturing, guiding, and ensuring the well-being of future generations—close human connections are formed individually and communally that can be intimate and transformative. It appears that several elements described in the literature are supportive of this study's finding that human relationships formed through giving back to society can be influential in creating meaning in later life.

Subtheme 4: Connections with Rekindled Relationships from the Past

An interesting and unexpected finding that emerged in the course of the study was the power and significance the participants experienced when reconnecting with others from their past. Marion speaks about the importance of renewing childhood relationships in terms of "closing the circle" and draws upon her pottery as a metaphor:

> Tell you what has given my life meaning, really I think of it in terms of pottery. You want to close your form. You want the form to have shape, but to be satisfying, the circle has to close. It's not satisfying to have an open circle like this. There's a tension.

Marion elaborates further with her personal experience at a high school reunion:

> My fiftieth high school reunion—no fortieth high school reunion, I finally went to. I hadn't gone to any in the past.... I connected with my four best friends from high school.... We were really fond—all of us were fond of all of us. We decided to meet the following year, just to get together the four. We live in five different cities. We've been meeting every year, since then, in a different city. That coming together with—bringing these threads of my early life back into my last life section has closed the circle and made a lot of meaning for me.

Ella also describes the impact of her reconnecting with a childhood friend and her family. She describes her emotional experience:

> When I retired, I had the ability to reconnect with my friend and her family. My friend's mom, may she rest in peace, ... would take the whole family on a cruise.... I could never justify taking a week off in

Human Relationships and Resiliency 55

January to do that, but when I retired I did. Then, I not only reconnected on a different level with my friend, we'd always stayed in touch, but it got deeper because we would spend seven days on a cruise ship with her mom and her brothers, and their wives and their children.... When I met her mom, (as a teenager) her mom said, "I just can't imagine that you haven't used the word mommy since you're 9 and a half years old." I was now 13, and she said, "Anytime you need to say it, just call me mommy." She treated me like ... she called me like her other daughter for years and years, and so reconnecting to her and then being in a place where I could say, "Mama J."; I couldn't do it when I was 13, I called her Mrs. L., but as I matured and understood really what a gift she had offered me, it just meant the most to me. When she died, her unveiling and everything, I was part of the family, she thought of me in that way. If hadn't retired when I did, I wouldn't have had that opportunity to reconnect with this beautiful family that was such an important part of my teenage years in particular.

The data indicate that the process of "closing the circle" through rekindling past relationships in later adulthood is a significant and impactful task. Marion explains: "We know each other's grandparents. Nobody in my (current) life, knew my father. No one. Not one person. I get together with these people and I can say, "Do you think I'm like my father?" The deep part of history is there and binds us very closely." Connecting with people who have a historical understanding of where we came from and where we are now is emotionally satisfying and seems to bring meaning to the arc of life.

Scholars within the literature have addressed this finding in an indirect manner. Many therapeutic interventions have developed that aim to help individuals discover the spiritual element that drives them to find ultimate meaning during their existence.[6] As mentioned previously, one such intervention entitled Life Review (LR) has had success with older adults.[7]

It appears LR and rekindling relationships from the past are based on the shared premise that connecting past experience with present life can enlarge one's sense of self and purpose. The findings of this study showed that when these reconnecting experiences are conducted in person, the meetings produce a great sense of satisfaction and fulfillment.

Superordinate Theme D: Resilience

The results of this study highlighted the important quality of resilience in making meaning in later life. During the course of a lifetime, there are

56 *Human Relationships and Resiliency*

many stresses, traumas, tragedies, and threats. The ability to endure and at some level recover from adversity allows one to continue to experience fulfillment in life. This ability to endure and come to terms with hardship and misfortune plays a significant role in integrating pain and sorrow while at the same time holding on to the dear parts of life. This study found four different life domains in which older adults' resiliency helped them feel positive about life in spite of the adversities often found in the aging process: medical problems, psychological problems, difficult life circumstances, and adapting to a changing world.

Subtheme 1: Medical Resilience

Many of the women in my sample have struggled with medical obstacles. For some, these physical problems are in their past while for others, they currently cope with physical limitations. In either case, their resiliency in dealing with past and current medical conditions has benefited them and allowed them to continue feeling that their lives continue to have purpose and meaning. Heidi, who still works as a CEO, contracted an infectious disease when she was an infant. She describes how this illness has impacted her current life:

> And then in my mid fifties I started falling and breaking limbs. And so now I can walk a block maybe a block-and-a-half. If I go to a museum and it's a lot to walk, I have to get into a wheelchair, I can't do it. I run a business and I would love to go to the sights and see the quality of the work that people are doing at the schools, at the preschools. If there are stairs I can't handle it, so I really have to know where I'm going first before I go. I'm very social, I used to go visit people, now I have to know what is your house like and can I come into it alone? Or do I have to call you when I get in your driveway and you have to give me a hand to get up the stairs?

At the same time that Heidi is acutely aware of her limitations and is at times angry about her circumstances, she continues her demanding 40-hour work week, which she finds gratifying and stimulating. Heidi describes her orientation towards life:

> I don't take life for granted. I don't waste days. If I'm sitting doing nothing it's because that's what I'm enjoying at that moment. I really enjoy my days and I'm really bothered by people who are just emotionally crippled and cannot even enjoy their good health, their luck in life, the things they have, I think I'd have no patience for it.

Human Relationships and Resiliency 57

Marion is another participant who has struggled with medical issues and at the same time continued to thrive in later adulthood. She describes her medical history:

> I've been quite sick. I had breast cancer when I was 38, and then when I was 39, I had cancer of the other breast. Each of them independent. Then, maybe 8 years ago, I had open-heart surgery for a leaky valve. I had a valve replaced. I'm not unacquainted with the reality of mortality. I'm not unacquainted at all. I feel like I'm on first-name terms with death.

At the same time that Marion has struggled with her health, faced death in the eye and felt the physical deterioration of aging, she has an on-going love for life. Her complaints get voiced in not having all the energy she would like to grab more of life:

> Age is affecting my energy level. I find after a full day, if I start at eight with a class, and then do this and do this, when I come home at five, I need a half an hour nap. Sometimes, I'll be out and just feel very tired, like I wanted to do this, I know I signed up for it, I know I wanted to, all I want to do is go home and rest. I do not have the energy that I used to have, but I had a very, very high energy level all my life.

Subtheme 2: Psychological Resilience

The thematic results from this study highlighted that those who can weather the emotional peaks and valleys in life seem to be equipped to lead purposeful and creative lives in later adulthood. The participants all spoke about past or present periods in their histories that have been emotionally painful. Nonetheless, all the participants seemed to feel that, even with these past or present hurts, they continue to lead lives that are fulfilling and creative. These women are able to think, feel, understand, and compartmentalize painful aspects of life such that they can also continue to find meaning in later adulthood.

Ella speaks about losing her mother when she was nine years old and how this has continued to impact her life. She says, "I'm also still that same insecure person that I was growing up because I was always different than everyone else because of my early trauma." She explains that due to her mother's death she always has "to do a lot of self-speak to get myself to do something I haven't done before." Further, she explains that she does

58   *Human Relationships and Resiliency*

not like to put herself "in a place where I might feel judged. It's all internal. That's my own stuff, but I'm well aware of that." At the same time that Ella is dealing with these internal struggles, she is aware of where her insecurities emanate, how they manifest themselves and how she self-soothes and copes during these times of insecurity. It would seem that this ability to navigate her own internal world gives her a psychological resiliency that allows for meaningful work, relationships, and experiences post-midlife. Bonnie speaks about her difficult childhood by explaining:

> My mother was completely nuts. I did not have the typical 1950s "Leave it to Beaver" childhood. She was in and out of psych hospitals. I think my first memory was going to visit her at a psych hospital.... When I was about 7 my parents divorced and God bless the judge. In those days you had to go to court. He gave custody to my father. She (my mother) was just completely self-centered and non-maternal. Didn't really get it. Luckily when I was like in about junior high, she ran out of the money that my father had given her. She went through it all so she moved back to Mexico and lived with her parents ... well, her mother and her stepfather until they died. Luckily she wasn't around so I had my father and Amalia (the housekeeper).

Bonnie seems to have had the ability to endure great pain and loss. Her psychological resilience has held her in good stead even post-midlife. While she did not have an involved mother herself she is intimately connected with her children, grandchildren, and extended family and derives great joy from these connections. She describes her satisfaction with all these connections: "My kids are lovely and they get along and their spouses are lovely and both spouses' fathers died but the two mother-in-laws are wonderful and we've become friends. Just hanging out with my kids. It's lovely." It appears that Bonnie's early loss did not significantly impact her ability to form close family ties. Once again, it is difficult to determine how and why some people are temperamentally stronger but this psychological resilience bodes well for meaning-making in later adulthood.

Subtheme 3: Resilience to Life Circumstances

Another type of resiliency stemmed from the ability to adjust to adverse life circumstances. Rose, for example, spoke about many past career stressors and present family frustrations in her life. In terms of career, Rose says:

Human Relationships and Resiliency 59

I think that the entire time that I was a school administrator I was incredibly stressed. I had pretty much a chronic cough, chronic constipation. I think it took a real toll on my health. After I stopped that job I did a lot of ... I got a trainer, I was exercising which is not something that I normally did. Went in and had a ton of tests. Just a lot of things that had backed up, but I don't feel that way anymore. My sleep too, I forgot to say, I was a complete insomniac for most of my life.... Yeah. I feel (today) mentally healthier and physically healthier.

Rose also spoke about her difficult relationship with her daughter, her responsibilities for her 98-year-old mother and disappointment with her siblings. She said, "You know when our daughter got a divorce, that was a very bad time for us. That particular daughter is pretty tough on me. Whatever it is, it's usually my fault." Also, Rose explained that although she has two local siblings, she takes most of the responsibility for their mother. "I see her (my mother) several times a week and I'm kind of on call." Her siblings do not help much with their mother. Further, they take her for granted and do not show appreciation:

Sometimes I get pretty aggravated at our siblings who seem in many ways to take advantage of us. That is a drag, that's a drag. We have a little guest house in the back and when they say they need to stay there for a month, or ... there's a lot of relatives. In March we had relatives probably at least 25 out of 30 days.

At the same time that Rose describes past and present difficult life circumstances, she maintains that her life has "a really nice balance of all these different segments that I wasn't able to ever pursue" previously. The resiliency to admit to life's painful situations at the same time as having the ability to experience the joys seems to be an important element in creating and maintaining meaning in later adulthood.

Bonnie, who used to work 60-hour work weeks as a doctor and knows that life can be short, spoke about her frustrations with her husband who refuses to cut back on his work or retire:

I think my husband makes me feel stuck and stagnant because he won't ... (retire). He doesn't get it. He doesn't get it.... He says he wants to take time off work and cut back but then he doesn't and then he's frustrated and I'm frustrated. Even though he's done very well and we have lots of money, he's not secure about it. For me that's very hard because it's frustrating. It's like, "Just enjoy it!" He doesn't enjoy it. We'll take a walk and I'll buy a $4 cup of latte and he doesn't

60 *Human Relationships and Resiliency*

want to buy a coffee. He thinks it's too much money. You make money in the long run doing that but there comes a point where you can spend $4 on a latte. Like last night was Purim, we talked about going to temple, but he comes home and he works and he's exhausted. I completely understand that because when I was working I would get up early, get there, I see 11 patients in the morning, maybe leave ... if I didn't bring my lunch and have it at my desk, I would run across the street and buy something at lunch, come back, see 11 patients, drive home through traffic, and then lay on that couch and I couldn't move. I get the exhaustion from working but that's why I retired. I retired because you can only do 24-hour shifts for so long.... He's now tired of being tired but not to the point where he made the conscious decision to work less.

Once again, however, even with Bonnie's frustrations with her life circumstances, she has shown resiliency. She explained how she is now traveling with friends and retired doctors since her husband is unavailable. She was invited by friends to take cooking classes in Italy and asked her husband:

You want to come cook in Italy? He said, "No." I said, "Bye!" It's the first time.

Well, I left him when I went to Vietnam. Same thing, I went with a doctor's group and I may do that again.

Additionally, she has filled her life with her children, grandchildren, and activities that speak to her personally. The fact that life circumstances preclude her from sharing these experiences with her husband has not stopped her from striving for meaning and purpose in her own life. This sort of resiliency to life circumstances seems to be an important factor in the meaning-making process in later adulthood.

Subtheme 4: Resilience to a Changing World

As people age, the world changes considerably from the one they knew as young adults. It seems there are two possible paths to navigating these changes. The first is to try to keep up with the continual changes in technology and knowledge. The other is to accept that the world has passed them by. It appears that those with the best resiliency come to accept what they can and cannot accomplish, as they grow older. Rose is an example of someone who saw the choices laid out in front of her and decided on which path she felt most comfortable. Rose was involved in teaching science and said she came to a fork in the road when she realized that:

Human Relationships and Resiliency 61

Things really change in science. I really did not feel current. I did not feel I did a good job of it. I've always been very enthusiastic about science. I love science and my enthusiasm can usually carry me through most any audience, just because I love it. I really felt like, things have changed and I've lost touch. I was not willing to take a class that was literally 12.5 hours a year. I wasn't willing to put in. I also would have taken 100 hours of work to maintain what I considered the knowledge to teach for 12.5 hours a year. Plus the whole computer thing happened and the on-line research. Everything about science changed so dramatically.

Rose weighed her priorities and interests and decided that she was not willing to put in the time to keep up with the ever-evolving world even though she still maintained a true love for science. She came up with a new path in which she would keep her passion for science alive through her travels, her active gardening work and research with succulents and her scientific experiences with her grandchildren. It appears that being resilient to worldly changes and finding paths to navigate these changes is an essential element in continuing to feel relevant and productive in later life.

Summary: Resilience

While it is difficult to ascertain how and why some people have more resilience than others, it does seem that those who have this quality are able to continue to find meaning in life in spite of their limitations and adverse circumstances. Resiliency as a construct has been more recently explored by researchers who challenge the idea that successful aging is no longer possible once health deteriorates and other negative life events occur. The literature regarding resiliency in older age concludes that good quality relationships, integration in the community, developmental coping and adaptive coping styles are protective attributes which allow for flourishing despite adversity.[8] A developmental coping style was defined as solution-driven and was equated with moving beyond adversity in a positive way. An adaptive coping style was defined as learning to live with a problem and thereby equated to integrating adversity. Further, resiliency was found to be either unrelated to (or related only weakly) to a person's socio-demographic characteristics.[9] While the literature does not address how and why some older people develop better coping styles than others, it does identify social engagement as associated with greater resiliency to meet adversity post-midlife.

Resilience is also addressed in the literature from an existential perspective. In Frankl's writings on search for meaning he proposed that

62 *Human Relationships and Resiliency*

people are more than biological, social, and psychological beings in that they have a spiritual element that drives them to find ultimate meaning during their existence.[10] Frankl maintained that there is a defiant power in the human spirit that can transcend the detrimental effects of stressful situations, illness, or the influences of the past. Based on these ideas, Frankl developed the therapeutic practice of logotherapy as a means to tap into the human spirit and find meaning in life in spite of adversity.

While neither the literature nor this study can completely explain the underpinnings of resiliency, being resilient appears to positively contribute to the older adult's ability to find meaning in later life. Even when faced with medical problems, psychological problems, difficult life circumstances, and/or the need to adapt to a changing world, having the ability to be resilient allows for continued growth and development in the later years.

Notes

1 Ruhl & Evans, 2014.
2 Corbett, 2014b.
3 Ibid.
4 Hollis, 2014.
5 Erikson, 1963; Ruhl & Evans, 2014; Corbett, 2014b.
6 Frankl, 1985.
7 Malette & Oliver, 2006.
8 Blane, Wiggins, Montgomery, Hildon, & Netuveli, 2011; Hildon, Montgomery, Blane, Wiggins, & Netuveli, 2010.
9 Blane et al., 2011.
10 Frankl, 1985.

5 Treatment Implications for Therapists Working with Older Adults

After listening to women's voices, one might ask about the treatment implications for therapists working with older adults. While I am reluctant to come up with a one-size fits-all model for treating older adults, I believe that some general ideas emerged from the study that may help professionals be more effective in their work.

Therapists Breathe in the Same Air

Therapists are not immune from breathing in the same cultural attitudes as the rest of the population. As such, the atmosphere in the treatment room can be infused with the stale navigational ideas that envision adults leaving middle age and beginning old age. This old map ignores the new space, created by longer lifespans, between middle age and old age. Although therapists may not be conscious of these outdated attitudes towards aging, it becomes their responsibility to look at themselves honestly and incorporate a more expanded vision for post-midlife adults. If a therapist's role is often to help a patient dream bigger and more expansively, it must begin in the intentional space that is co-created between patient and therapist. When a therapist has integrated this new development stage, whether it be the "third act, third chapter, or encore stage," he or she is in a better position to help patients grow into this next developmental milestone. Once the therapist has adjusted to this new developmental stage, he or she will be better able to address the details that appear to be most significant in creating a meaningful and purposeful life in later adulthood.

Existential Pursuits

In working clinically with adults post-midlife, it is important for the clinician to understand the existential pursuits that are developmentally pertinent to creating a meaningful life in later adulthood:

64   *Therapists Working with Older Adults*

1   Gaining a deeper understanding of the self as a means to develop unused potential.
2   Acquainting oneself with the concept of death as a means to live life more fully.
3   Fostering a spiritual connection through experiences that feed the soul and nourish the spirit.
4   Leaving a legacy/sharing wisdom as a means to leave something of oneself behind in this world and make a difference through one's own actions.

Given that modern society has glorified youth, many clients come to psychotherapy with the idea that their lives are no longer relevant and that they must settle into lowering their expectations for their future. Psychoeducation may be required to help clients understand that older adulthood has new benefits, gifts, and responsibilities. While there must be an acceptance of the losses that take place, part of the clinical work may entail enlarging clients' vision of themselves and their possible contributions to society at large.

Affirmation of Life

When working with older adults, clinicians will benefit from understanding the need for clients to incorporate life-affirming activities, as they are an important element in creating and maintaining a purposeful life. Life-affirming activities can be categorized as cognitively, creatively, or physically stimulating and challenging endeavors. Additionally, encouraging elders to adopt a learning stance towards life provides the opportunity to benefit from life-long learning. Although clients may be retired or moving in that direction, it remains essential for these older adults to remain engaged in life. While the responsibilities of life may change with age, the need for exciting, thought-provoking, and invigorating endeavors remains an important feature for obtaining fulfillment in later life.

Human Relationships

Clinicians must be aware that the need for human connection follows people throughout the lifespan. Connections with family, friends, community, and rekindled relationships from youth serve as an important foundation for feeling part of the human family. The idea of settling into a quiet life with little human contact is a formula for disaster for older adults. Clinicians should be aware of this important developmental task, particularly in light of the possible loss of family and friends. It is

Therapists Working with Older Adults 65

important for the individual in the second half of life to retain the ability to form new friendships as a means to cope with a world that might feel like it is shrinking.

Resiliency

Clinicians treating older adults must be prepared to assess their clients' resiliency to face the challenges that arise from medical, psychological, and situational circumstances. When resiliency is weakened by negative life events, the clinician should consider working on existential issues and coping skills. Existential work along the lines of logotherapy and LR can serve as a means to seek, locate, and energize the client's human spirit. Strengthening coping skills would focus on developing tools to either move beyond or integrate adverse life situations. Lastly, helping clients create and maintain social engagement is particularly important in increasing older adults' resiliency.

6   Where Do We Go from Here?

After all is said and done, where do we go from here? It becomes apparent, from listening to women speak about their later years in life, that the ability to retain creative authorship of one's life and narrative is paramount to finding purpose and meaning. The ability to feel that one can continue to give, receive, and be a significant contributor in one's personal world and the world at large has a staggering effect on feeling vital and included. But, how can this be achieved? While modern medicine has enabled individuals to live longer, this medical feat has not been matched by society's ability to redefine the later years. Seeing people entering their seventh and eighth decade as expendable, over-the-hill, and no longer viable members of society, when they may live into their ninth decade and beyond, can have devastating consequences on multiple levels of human existence: the *intrapersonal level*, the *interpersonal level* and the *societal level*. The search to conceptualize anew this stage of later life must therefore direct attention to all three levels of our existence.

The Intrapersonal Level

What allows people in their later years to see themselves as creative and purposeful? While I have tried to steer clear of the autobiographical in this book, the inner mental workings upon which I have the firmest grasp are undoubtedly my own. Given the inherent limitation on fully entering others' inner worlds, I draw upon my own life experience to understand this intrapersonal level. The forces that propelled me to embark upon the doctoral degree I completed at the age of 62 years are emblematic of the driving force within people to continue to grow and develop throughout the lifespan. First, however, let's look at human development in general.

From the moment we are born, we are each aging and losing aspects of ourselves. The infant loses the breast as he or she begins to eat proper food; the school-age child loses the continuous physical proximity and

Where Do We Go from Here? 67

protection of his or her parents or caretakers when introduced to a larger more dynamic environment; the college student is asked to move even farther away from family, physically and metaphorically, so that he or she can develop into a fully-functioning adult and acquire the gifts of intimate relationships, careers, and family. This cycle continues throughout the life-span, with painful loses continually creating vacuums that need attention. When all goes well, the empty painful spaces are filled and at least partially resolved with meaning-making opportunities. This is, in fact, what transpired for me personally as my fifth and youngest child left home for college when I was in my late fifties.

After so many years of mothering, the empty nest left me feeling unbalanced and directionless. And so, with that loss, the painful vacuum was created and I was forced to look at what's next in my life, if life was to have any purpose or meaning going forward. My children no longer needed me in the same way but I was accustomed to a busy household filled with tremendous activity and stimulation. With my last child set to leave home and my husband busy in his own fulfilling career, I was at a loss in so many different ways. I had always dreamed of pursuing doctoral studies in psychology and deepening my level of understanding of the human psyche. I already was a licensed clinical social worker, but had stopped working many years ago to tend to all my children. This was perhaps the right time to pursue the dream. But, a nagging voice within me kept asking: Who would want a doctoral student who was starting this enormous project in her late fifties? This question ended up being my own "self-ageism," for it certainly did not play out in my life. First of all, my husband and friends were entirely supportive. One friend in particular said, "G-d willing you will turn 62 one way or the other so why not with the title 'Doctor' attached to your name?" He turned my doubts upside down by challenging me to fill my life with meaning.

Even after I began my doctoral work, the doubts continued: Would I be able to function academically after all these years and be able to write a dissertation? Would anyone hire me to do clinical work as a practicum student or offer me an internship after my coursework was complete? The questions and doubts continued to plague me as I successfully jumped through the hoops of coursework, clinical work, and dissertation.

The journey has been eminently "worth it" so far. So how does one convert loss and pain to opportunity at this stage in life? It seems to be a process of listening to one's dreams that have been muted, and surrounding oneself with all the support possible. For me, developing my professional identity was a pursuit that had been ignored and dismissed in order to be a fully supportive wife and mother. The time had come to develop these as-yet undeveloped aspects of myself. This is exactly what Jung

68   *Where Do We Go from Here?*

envisioned in the "second half of life"—a time to focus upon the hidden aspects of self.

While I still struggle with my own personal ageism along with my other inner demons, the process seems to require risk-taking and allowing for the idea that older adults' accumulated life experience and wisdom is marketable, useful, and even necessary. The inner voices that belittled my own personal growth and development are certainly not unique to me. Some of those doubts emanate from personal insecurity, but many come from a culture that glorifies youth and leaves older adults feeling that they should be in retreat. This cultural message serves as an undertow that drags older adults beneath its harsh current with the message for them to pull back, minimize and disengage once their age starts with the numeral 6. Challenging these cultural messages about what is "age appropriate" for older adults must be done intra-psychically in addition to addressing the message in the outside world. We must each come to see these later years as a time filled with possibility and opportunity. We must personally expand our vision of what it means to continue to find meaning in later life.

As the women in my study show, there are role models aplenty, but we must look towards them and block out the negative cultural norms and stereotypes that are implicitly internalized and embodied over the course of the lifespan.[1] These internalized stereotypes become a barrier to expansion and suggest that life must close down as one grows older. Rather, the new message must be that the show does not stop until we have breathed our last breath. If we were given these extra years of life, there must be a reason; we owe ourselves the opportunity to explore, learn, and grow as long as we are capable.

The Interpersonal Level

Once again, I pose the question: What allows people in their later years to be creative and purposeful? While working on the intrapersonal level is an essential step to expand one's dreams and aspirations in later life, humans do not grow and develop within a vacuum. Growth and development has always relied on interpersonal connection and relationships. As infants, we have an inborn need to bond with parents and caregivers in order to physically thrive and develop. As we grow, human connection is the fuel that energizes all activity without diminishing as we age. This need for human connection burns strongly throughout the lifespan. Our need to give to others and our need to receive from others is part of our basic humanity that courses through our bloodstream. Our neurology itself depends on the oxytocin that is released when one feels cared about and has physical

Where Do We Go from Here? 69

contact. Being seen, acknowledged, touched, and cared about is imprinted in our souls, minds, and bodies.

For older adults, the ability to draw excitement, passion, and adventure in later years demands additional relationships that cross traditional borders. As an example, I draw upon my own experience recounted above, namely returning to school for doctoral studies in my late fifties. My doctoral program was set up so that I took all my classes with the same group of students for the entire four years of coursework. Additionally, the program was residential—once a month, for four very full days, the nine people in my cohort ate meals together, slept in the same motel together, and studied and socialized together. I was the oldest student in the cohort, the youngest student being 30 years my junior and the mean age 20 years younger.

While returning to school and studying was an exhilarating experience, perhaps even more significant was the learning that took place through these intergenerational relationships. The first day I walked on campus, I was directed by a fellow-student to join the class Facebook group, a social media of which I was only dimly aware. Going forward, my younger classmates helped me understand how to make PowerPoint presentations, use software to help with my dissertation research, and generally to be more agile with my personal computer. But these are just the superficial gifts I received. My mind was opened regarding how they think about gender, sexuality, politics, entertainment, and much more. I looked forward to my monthly school weekends not just for the classes but for the sense of vitality and life that these relationships engendered. Further, I believed that I not only received from these relationships but also gave in return.

Cohorts are a tricky business, often subject to dark, ugly periods in which relationships become messy and uncomfortable. Unlike most relationships, however, the cohort afforded no ability to walk away and make distance—short of dropping out of the program. And there were those who actually did drop out when the intensity rose. When things were at their worst, the cohort decided we needed a student representative; they asked me to take the helm. There was a sense that I had the emotional maturity to lead the group out of chaos. The group seemed to sense that my number of years on the planet imparted a level of life experience, wisdom, and patience that would be helpful in navigating through the stormy period. It also gave me a sense of purpose and the delight of feeling needed. My strengths were noticed, acknowledged, and utilized.

I rely upon my own personal experience in school as I believe it is indicative of a larger phenomenon. The idea is that older adults must push themselves outside their comfort zones and experience relationships with people who are different from themselves simply to remain vibrant and

70   *Where Do We Go from Here?*

alive. These differences can be age, race, religion, personality type, or some other variable that allows for different interpersonal experiences. These relationships allow older adults to expand their thinking about others and themselves and serve as energy to propel growth, learning, and development. Sarah Lawrence-Lightfoot speaks about these experiences as "boundary crossings" that instigate new learning. She sees "boundary crossings" in many ways—"crossing disciplinary boundaries, crossing the boundaries between art and science, crossing generational boundaries, crossing geographic boundaries, crossing the boundaries of race and class, crossing gender boundaries, and crossing the boundaries between work and play." Lawrence-Lightfoot explains that as older adults navigate new borders:

> They are forced to learn new skills, take on different temperamental styles, try on new personas, learn how they learn, and reinvent themselves. In navigating these boundaries people begin to enlarge their repertoire, their range of choices, perspectives, and frameworks—their ways of being in the world. They become more layered and multidimensional.[2]

There is a paradox here, though. As older adults are given the cultural message to make their worlds smaller by pulling back, minimizing, and disengaging, they in fact are in desperate need of expanding their worlds. In order to take advantage of this life stage in which one is neither too old nor too young, when transformation and generativity is not only possible but desirable, older adults need access to relationships that cross traditional borders. And so, we turn to the *societal level*.

The Societal Level

We once again begin with the same question from a different angle: How can society encourage individuals in their later years to be creative and purposeful? The primary answer to this question is the need to redefine the post-midlife years. While medicine has created longer lifespans, society has not kept up with what this means for the people who are living longer. We are using an old map instead of upgrading to a GPS that recognizes adults no longer leave middle age and begin old age. There now is a new space between middle age and old age that has been ignored. Our culture and institutions continue to see younger people as the primary segment of society that has energy, drive, and new ideas. Further, society has not seen older age as a time of great opportunity for generativity and transformation. Nor has society appreciated the beauty, wisdom, and experience that

Where Do We Go from Here? 71

comes with life experience. In short, the current understanding of aging has not kept pace with older adults' abilities, talents, and gifts. This narrow view of aging, in fact, keeps not just older adults confined but society at large hostage. The idea of being burdened with more dependents has gained more attention than the idea of drawing upon older adults to continue to contribute to society through work, volunteering, mentoring, social action, intergenerational relationships, and more. Further, the idea of young and old working and learning together, as opposed to competing for access, opportunity, and resources, has not been given serious attention. Currently, economic and public policy perspectives have created an adversarial relationship between young and old such that they see themselves competing for resources and services. Marc Freedman calls this new life period *The Encore Stage* and argues that, just as adolescence, middle age and parenthood have become recognized life stages with their own experts, advice literature, and niche magazines, this stage of life needs to be reimagined.[3] Freedman says that:

> The remapping of life's categories is rarely an orderly, or linear, process. There is no reason to think that this new life stage will be any different. This process entails a messy break from old patterns of thinking that compromise our ability to reimagine the period between midlife and old age. That means resisting the temptation to see this time as a version of something else—whether that's endless midlife or reinvented retirement. Once we break free of old ideas, we need to replace them, with something else. That means launching the new stage with a dream for this period, a new definition of "success" and new language and branding to establish the integrity and weight of this time of life.[4]

In an attempt to define and structure this new life stage that stands between midlife and old age, Freedman proposes a number of measures that might begin to carry society into this new territory:[5]

- *A gap year for grown-ups.* Freedman suggests that a gap year could serve as a preparation for a new stage of personal meaning and productive contribution. This year would be a time to ponder questions about what "new growth" is ready to germinate in this season of your life? It would also provide time to build a new foundation for this growth.
- *Highest education.* The education suited to this stage of life would have the goal of "paving the way to a new stage of productive contribution." There are already some models of this educational approach

72 *Where Do We Go from Here?*

such as The Advanced Leadership Initiative at Harvard and various community colleges around the country that are focused upon helping those over 50 navigate a path that can combine vocational preparation, personal transformation, and intellectual stimulation.

- *Paying for the encore.* Freedman realizes that most Americans are not in the position to self-fund a gap year or pay tuition for further education. He suggests that there needs to be public and private sector solutions that will help those entering the encore years to regroup for a productive new chapter in their lives. He suggests two possible strategies: Individual Purpose Accounts and an "Encore Bill" akin to the G.I. Bill.
- *The freedom to work.* According to Freedman, most older people need or want to work longer but they are at the same time ready for a change. Encore careers often focus upon channeling older adults' experience in the direction of improving the community and the world at large. In general, the idea is to change the perception from freedom from work to freedom to work in ways that are personally meaningful and a merit to society. This shift will need "encore friendly" employment policies that include flextime for aging parents, part-time job and on-the-job skills training. Most importantly, subtle and not-so-subtle age discrimination in hiring needs to be addressed.

In order for society to address this new life stage it will require new ways of thinking about the years between midlife and old age. It will also require innovations in social infrastructure and public policies. In order to avert what some call the "silver tsunami" in which longevity is seen as a burden on society we need to reimagine and support a new version of this life stage. In so doing, society will be able tap into the talent, experience, and wisdom of many older adults and thereby promote greater personal happiness and societal good. Currently, older adults who are capable of making meaningful changes in their lives are on a do-it-yourself path that is possible due to certain economic advantages. In order to allow a larger swathe of older adults to find purpose, meaning, and give back to society, we need to foster their growth on a societal level.

Notes

1 Swift, Abrams, Lamont, & Drury, 2017.
2 Lawrence-Lightfoot, 2009, p. 141.
3 Freedman, 2011.
4 Freedman, 2014, p. 103.
5 Ibid., pp. 103–111.

7 Final Thoughts
Big Data, Depth Psychology, and Poetry

> Aging is not merely about the body losing its poise, strength, and self-trust. Aging also invites you to become aware of the sacred circle that shelters your life. Within the harvest circle, you are able to gather lost moments and experiences, bring them together, and hold them as one. In actual fact, if you can come to see aging not as the demise of your body but as the harvest of your soul, you will learn that aging can be a time of great strength, poise and confidence.
>
> John O'Donohue[1]

The words above were written by an Irish poet, author, priest, and Hegelian philosopher who was best known for popularizing Celtic spirituality. It is uncanny to see how O'Donohue's writing captures the voices of the women in my study. His prose caused me to pause and question: How do we know what we know?

Big Data vs. In-Depth Data

Shortly after completing the qualitative study described in this book, I had nagging concerns about the legitimacy of my results. After all, the world has come to embrace big data—elaborate statistical analyses performed on quantitative data derived from mega-samples. The mathematical gymnastics involved in these quantitative empirical studies have all the drama of an aerial stunt performer who shows no signs of difficulty with the feat. Did my coffee table conversations, although rich, textured, and full of intimate sharing that yielded in-depth data, hold the same credibility? While I understood that all *quantitative* data is operationalized such that most if not all nuance and explanatory ability is squeezed out of the process, my concerns lingered: What about my *qualitative* data? Did the small homogeneous sample required by Interpretative Phenomenological Analysis really get to

74 *Final Thoughts*

the crux of finding meaning in later life? Did women's descriptions of life getting better as they matured really hold water?

Given these concerns, it was with great interest that, one month after analyzing the results of my study, I opened the *Los Angeles Times* to find an article describing a University of California, San Diego study entitled "The Aging Paradox: The Older We Get, The Happier We Are."[2] The title of this article seemed drawn right out of my participants' mouths! As you read above (p. 33), one participant shared her feelings about *how* age affects emotional contentment:

> I thought, you know, when you're younger—the worst decades in my life, I think, were supposed to be the best. My teen years, my twenties, even early thirties, were times of tremendous stress. I realize now it's because I was creating my life. I didn't know. I didn't know what would be. There was tremendous anxiety and need to define myself, and to prove myself, and to make these crucial life decisions. Everything depended on these crucial life decisions. Now, it's much better. Much, much better. Those decisions are in the past, they've been made, there's no changing it. How do you find meaning? At this point in your life, you see the arc of your life. You can tell the story of your life. Whereas, the early years, you're so busy writing it that you can't see it.

I quickly got hold of the study itself, in order to review the scholarly version for myself.[3] Whereas my study focused on six women as participants, this study boasted a sample size of 1,546 men and women, aged 21–100 years, who were all randomly selected. The data included self-report measures of physical health, measures of both positive and negative attributes of mental health, and a phone interview-based measure of cognition. Its findings, according to the researchers:

> Support the existence of a "paradox" in which aging is associated with better mental health among older adults at the population level despite loss of physical and cognitive function ... [The researchers *hypothesize* about their statistical findings by suggesting] that an important explanation for improved mental health in later life is an increase in wisdom with aging, as suggested by several studies. Other studies have also reported that, compared to younger adults, older individuals tend to be more skilled at emotional regulation and complex social decision-making and tend to exhibit more positively valenced information processing ... These behavioral changes parallel functional imaging studies showing diminished responsiveness of the amygdala to negative or stressful images in older compared to younger adults. Such positivity may lead to higher levels of subjective well-being in later life.[4]

Final Thoughts 75

To my delight, these quantitative studies mirrored my own qualitative results: Instead of the polynomial regressions of that study, my study featured women's own voices explaining the phenomenon and sharing *how* they were making their lives purposeful and meaningful. Quantitative studies are typically observational, meaning that they cannot expose the mechanism of the observed phenomenon. Qualitative studies such as IPA have smaller samples, are less experimental in nature, but share the actual voices and narratives of people who are living through the process under examination. Certainly, each design has its own strengths and weaknesses—but, taken together, they can become a mighty force.

Laura Carstensen, director of the Stanford Center on Longevity, also found an improvement in emotional well-being among older adults in her longitudinal study.[5] The participants in her study were people in which ethnicity, gender, and socioeconomic status were stratified across age. The data were collected in three different waves (1993–1995, 1998–2001, and 2004–2005) with nearly 200 people tracked over 10 years of their lives. The data were generated through questionnaires that assessed physical health, personality, happiness, and cognitive ability. Although Carstensen recognized the inability to explain her findings, she hypothesized that "constraints on time horizons result in the chronic activation of goals related to emotional meaning."[6] In other words, as people age and realize that their time on earth is finite, their focus shifts to emotionally meaningful goals and negative emotions become less frequent and more fleeting.

Once again, I was excited to see the close parallels between my qualitative study and this large quantitative study. In my study, a participant gave personal testimony to Carstensten's hypothesis. When I asked one of my participants whether she harbored fear towards her eventual death she responded: "No, my husband's 76. I'm 73. We could die tomorrow. I'm not afraid of his dying. I'm not afraid of my dying." The participant does speak, however, about the idea of death serving as a motivator. She says, "It makes me anxious to get done what I want to get done ... because there's a deadline. You've got a deadline. You get energized right before your deadline, right?"

Big data serves a purpose, no doubt about it. But qualitative data animates the cold numbers, giving voice to the numbers and statistics generated by quantitative studies. The two research designs support and complement each other. The idea that qualitative research does not possess scientific rigor, however, can no longer be sustained.

Depth Psychology

Depth psychologists, such as James Hillman and Carl Jung, look at aging from a different perspective than scholars and researchers who study

76   *Final Thoughts*

"successful aging." Successful age researchers focus on warding off normal biological declines associated with the aging process; as a result, they define success as having good to excellent health, no disabilities in activities of daily living, good cognitive functioning, and living in the community.[7] Depth psychologists view the tableau from a wholly different perspective. They look at later life as a summons to internal growth, personal development, and spiritual awakening. When interviewed at age 74, James Hillman contended that it "is not our hips that need replacing, but our beliefs about old age—ideas that give priority to biology and economics, rather than to soul and individual character."[8] For Hillman, character and soul are the primary aspects of being human; he thus contends that as individuals mature, they are given the opportunity to develop and grow their unique and essential selves. For Hillman, each wrinkle on the face and battle wound of life is a badge of honor that has the possibility of signifying an elevated soul. Hillman counsels older adults to keep their eyes open to both the "fading light and the blaze of beauty at sunset."[9] Hillman's version of "successful aging" therefore involves letting go of useless negative ideas about aging and finding its inherent value. He further suggests that society does not:

> Realize the practical value of older people. We attribute to them old age wisdom and sagacity and all these good things, but we don't have much use for that in our get-up-and-go culture. We have to realize that old people are very practical for society: they know a lot; they've acquired many skills; they have a knowledge of tools. Think of old carpenters, old gardeners. An old cloth merchant in New York City can touch a material and know what it's all about and that's practical. We need to look at old people more practically in order to restore their value. Maybe they don't know computers, but there is more to life than computers. What about eating and cooking? What about having an eye for people, knowing how to handle feelings?[10]

Hillman teaches us that older age comes with skills and gifts that are often not appreciated by those who have reached their later years nor by society at large. The need to look beyond the surface of youthful energy and beauty, to embrace the deepening of character of older adults has been neglected and undervalued.

Carl Jung and his followers also saw "the second half of life" as an opportunity for spiritual growth, meaning, and purpose. Whereas the first half of life, according to Jung, is governed by building family and career, Jung theorized that the second half of life is characterized by greater engagement with philosophical and spiritual issues. Those who have

Final Thoughts 77

expanded on Jung's ideas see later adulthood as a time to develop one's unused potential and take on new roles and responsibilities in society. Jung also saw death as a great motivator to make the most of life. Jung was interviewed in 1959, two years before his death at age 86:

FREEMAN: You have told us that we should regard death as the only goal.

JUNG: Yes.

FREEMAN: And to shrink away from it is to evade life and to make life purposeless?

JUNG: Yes.

FREEMAN: What advice would you give to people in later life to enable them to do this?

JUNG: I have treated many old people and it is quite interesting to watch what the unconscious is doing with the fact that it is apparently threatened with a complete end. It disregards it—life behaves as if it were going on, and I think it better for old people to live on—to look forward to the next day, as if he had to spend centuries, and then he lives properly. But when he is afraid he doesn't look forward, he looks back, he petrifies, he gets stiff and dies before his time; but when he is living on, looking forward to the great adventure that is ahead, then he lives ...[11]

Depth psychology's ideas and practice have often been dismissed for failing to be "evidenced-based." The rationale is that if ideas cannot be measured and quantified, then they are not worth pondering, considering, or taking as serious data. In the face of that prejudice, it is fascinating to see how closely the ideas of these depth psychologists dovetail with the quantitative studies described earlier. The results in my qualitative study likewise found that many older adults feel graced by the gifts of later adulthood, seeing it as a very meaningful and purposeful stage of life.

The take-home message here is that we need to listen to and honor the spiritual and soulful aspects of human existence in later life as they are a rich source of data and knowledge. The idea that "true science" should ignore what can't be measured is a means to minimize our humanity. Further, the idea that empiricism holds the ultimate truth in fact obscures the truth. Human existence and older adulthood must be understood using all the dimensions of our knowledge, including our senses and intuition. It is only through including these depth psychological approaches that we can continue to hear the spirit and honor the soul of humankind.

78   *Final Thoughts*

Poetry

Just as depth psychology taps into dimensions of knowing that are intuitively sensed and understood, the humanities, including writers, artists, and poets, bring another dimension to understanding life in all its complicated forms. When we use the phrase "life imitating art" we see the inherent intermingling of human existence and sensual, aesthetic, knowing and expression. Poetry aims to minimize words and find the essence of nature in all its forms. Poetry also has the ability to use aesthetic means to wake us up and remind us what is unique, special, and underappreciated. As I end this book, I can find no better words to remind us of the gifts of older adulthood and the need to respect all sources of knowledge than a poem by John O'Donohue:

> May the light of your soul mind you,
> May all of your worry and anxiousness about becoming old be transfigured,
> May you be given a wisdom with the eye of your soul, to see this beautiful time of harvesting.
> May you have the commitment to harvest your life, to heal what has hurt you, to allow it to come closer to you and become one with you.
> May you have great dignity, may you have a sense of how free you are,
> and above all may you be given the wonderful gift of meeting the eternal light and beauty that is within you.
> May you be blessed, and may you find a wonderful love in yourself for yourself.[12]

Notes

1 O'Donohue, 1997, pp. 167–168.
2 Netburn, 2016.
3 Thomas et al., 2016.
4 Ibid., p. e1023.
5 Carstensen et al., 2011.
6 Ibid., p. 29.
7 Hillman, 1999; Jung, 1960; Jorm et al., 1998.
8 Zeiger, 2000.
9 Ibid., p. 2.
10 Ibid., p. 4.
11 Freeman, 1989, p. 60.
12 O'Donohue, 1997, p. 198.

Appendix A
Methodology

Research Approach

The research approach utilized in this book, exploring how post-midlife individuals shape meaningful lives, was a qualitative design. While quantitative research methodologies have often been associated with rigorous research, that include double blind randomized controlled trials (RCT), equally rigorous yet distinctive qualitative designs have found a niche in the study of social phenomena and psychology.[1] Over the last two decades qualitative approaches have become widely accepted in the field of psychology.[2] Qualitative approaches, in contrast to quantitative research, have the advantage of allowing in-depth and detailed study of experiences that are not easily quantifiable.[3] Further, the qualitative approach is uniquely designed to explore and understand the *meaning* individuals and groups assign to human experiences and social problems.[4] Additionally, qualitative inquiry uniquely honors efforts made at studying complex life experiences from a personal perspective.[5] In summary, the attributes of qualitative research allow the researcher to create a richer description of the phenomenon under investigation. As such, a qualitative approach was appropriate to further understand how individuals continue to find meaning by creating satisfying and creative life experiences at the same time that their chronological age increases.

Research Methods

The research for this book utilized Interpretive Phenomenological Analysis (IPA) as its research method. IPA is known as a qualitative method for data analysis of social phenomena.[6] Currently, IPA is widely used within British psychology.[7] Jonathan Smith developed IPA in the mid-1990s by using a theory that originated with the philosopher Edmund Husserl.[8] Husserl attempted to construct a philosophical science of

80   Appendix A: Methodology

consciousness, with hermeneutics and with social interactionism.[9] In other words his work endeavored to join the theory of interpretation with symbolic interactionism—a school of thought that posits that the meanings an individual ascribes to events are of great import but are only accessible through an interpretative process. Consequently, IPA recognizes that the researcher's engagement with the participants' texts has an interpretative element that allows the researcher to access an individual's cognitive inner world.[10]

Smith differentiated IPA from other phenomenological research in that IPA recognizes the central role of the research analyst as an interpreter of participants' personal experience.[11] This researcher/interpreter role explains the strong connection between IPA and the interpretative or hermeneutic tradition.[12] Due to IPA researchers' active participation and interpretation, IPA has recognized that this model of human research involves a double hermeneutic. The double hermeneutic can be seen as the experiential synthesis between researcher and participant derived from participants trying to make sense of their personal and social world and researcher trying to make sense of the participants trying to make sense of their personal and social world.[13]

Smith asserted that IPA operates at a level which is grounded in the participant's words but which also moves beyond the participant's words to a more interpretative and psychological level.[14] Smith claimed that the researcher has different levels of interpretation available. This ability to interpret on different levels contributes to the distinctive and creative characteristics of qualitative psychology. Further, these interpretations also map closely to the complex reality of psychological process.[15] To illustrate the different levels of analysis Smith worked on the short extract below which was extracted from a study of the personal experience of chronic benign lower back pain.

> During an interview discussing this, one woman, Linda, says: I just think I'm the fittest because there are three girls and I'm the middle one and I thought well I'm the fittest and I used to work like a horse and I thought I was the strongest and then all of a sudden it's just been cut down and I can't do half of what I used to do.[16]

Smith contended that there are at least three levels of interpretation consonant with IPA for the passage above.[17] At the first level, Linda was absorbed in a social comparison with her sisters. At the second level, Linda used metaphor by comparing herself to a horse. Smith interpreted this horse metaphor as the vehicle Linda used to exaggerate her past strength in order to emphasize the weakness she felt at the time of the

Appendix A: Methodology 81

interview. Smith used his own metaphor in describing the "fine grained" third level of analysis. He explained that at this third level the interpreters should look at the change in tense from "*I'm* the fittest" to "I *thought* I was the strongest." Smith continued his explanation of this change in tense:

> This seems to confirm that Linda is referring to a time in the past when she had such great strength and which she has now lost. So how does one explain the apparent contradiction—"I am the fittest," "I was the fittest"? Well I think this goes to the heart of the psychological battle for Linda, as her sense of identity is ravaged by her back pain. Thus, on the one hand, Linda acknowledges that she has lost an identity—a strong, proud and autonomous self, which has been replaced by an enfeebled and vulnerable self. On the other hand, Linda still "identifies" with the strong self—so that in part her sense of who she is is still represented by the superfit being in the image. Thus Linda is struggling between being taken over by a new self, *defined* by her chronic pain and hanging on to an old self, *in spite of* that pain. This struggle is literally illustrated in the temporal changes in the passage itself.[18]

Smith clarified the bounds of IPA by explaining why he rejected a fourth level of analysis that was offered to him.[19] This interpretation was that the horse symbolized Linda's sexual appetite, frustrated by her current condition. Smith believed that this interpretation illustrates the difference between a grounded IPA reading and an imported psychoanalytic one. Smith explained that this interpretation of the horse relies upon the use of a formal extant theory, which is then read into the passage, whereas his interpretations were based on a close reading of what is already in the text.

As clearly demonstrated by Smith, IPA requires the researcher to look beyond the words and distill the meaning behind them.[20] As such, this method proved to be an excellent vehicle to explore the subject matter of meaning in the aging process because IPA allowed the researcher to explore in detail how participants were making sense of their personal and social world.[21] The use of IPA was also appropriate in that it was idiographic and thereby allowed the researcher to explore each participant's personal perspective prior to moving to more general claims regarding the phenomena under examination.[22] By using IPA for this study, individuals were able to share personal perspectives on their aging process. Further, when the data collected was looked at cumulatively, further information was shed on the variables and attitudes that propelled individuals to continue living in the deepest sense. In summary, IPA methodology was appropriate for studying meaning-making post-midlife as it is a particularly

82 Appendix A: Methodology

effective method for studying "dynamic, contextual and subjective, and relatively under-studied topics where issues relating to identity, the self and sense making are investigated."[23]

Participants

Given that IPA is an idiographic approach that is concerned with understanding particular phenomena in particular contexts, the study was conducted on a small, homogeneous sample in which the research question was relevant. In accordance with this orientation, a sample of six participants was selected purposively and found through the researcher's professional contacts and participants' referrals. Inclusion criteria for the participants was individuals aged 60 and over who were verbal, reflective, and interested in exploring how they were navigating this time in their lives. Individuals were excluded if their life circumstances did not favor this line of investigation. The researcher utilized gatekeepers of professional organizations to first approach potential participants with an invitation to participate. After potential participants agreed to contact with researcher, the researcher contacted these individuals directly and explained the aim of the research study with verbatim instructions. Potential participants were then screened by phone prior to being enlisted in the study to ensure that they met the inclusion criterion (see Appendix B for Screening Guide). At the end of this process the sample was selected and was comprised of six married women between the ages of 63 and 73. All the participants had been married between 36 and 50 years, had adult children and were grandparents. This sample met IPA's standards and "represent a perspective, rather than a population."[24] Participants were experts on their own aging experience who could provide the researcher a detailed understanding of their inner world.

Data Collection

Potential participants were approached by phone and screened by using a screening guide. Additionally, the aim of the research study was explained to them along with confidentiality arrangements. If the potential participant seemed appropriate, an interview was set up during this initial phone contact. Data was collected through face-to-face, semi-structured interviews at a location of their choosing, that lasted between 60–90 minutes. These interviews had the flavor of a "conversation with an intention." The interview was guided by some questions that arose from the literature review (see Appendix B for Interview Guide). Nonetheless the interviews remained flexible in order to allow for unanticipated topics to emerge. In particular, the researcher was interested in exploring how individuals were

Appendix A: Methodology 83

creating and living meaningful, productive, and even transcendent lives post-midlife. Interviews were recorded and transcribed verbatim.

Data Analysis

The data from the semi-structured interviews was analyzed using IPA stages: Immersion, Transformation, Labeling, and Organization.[25]

1 *Immersion*: The first step of immersion required the researcher to read the whole transcript from the interview several times, getting the flavor of the participant's words and taking notes of initial impressions. The subsequent step of immersion was performing a line-by-line analysis of the participant's experience as articulated in the transcript.

2 *Transformation*: At this stage the notes taken during the immersion stage were transformed into emerging themes or concepts that emphasized "convergence and divergence, commonality and nuance."[26] Further, during the Transformation stage, Smith's ideas about finding different levels of interpretation began to unfold and the researcher was asked to make interpretations while not losing connection to the participants' own words.[27] This process required the researcher to have a dialogue with the coded data in order to determine what it might mean for participants to have these concerns and claims. The researcher benefited from the aid of qualitative research software (Dedoose) designed for analyzing qualitative data.

3 *Labeling*: This step required the attachment of a descriptive label to each theme or pattern that emerged from the data. This was an attempt to "develop a structure, frame, or gestalt which illustrated the relationship between themes."[28]

4 *Organization*: At this stage the themes derived from the Labeling stage above were analyzed and organized into superordinate themes and subthemes that corresponded to the researcher's thought process and interpretations. Developing a table of themes helped show "the structure of major themes and subthemes. Illustrative data excerpts were presented along to the side of each theme, followed by the line number which made returning to the transcript and checking the quotation in context possible."[29]

The table of themes was the outcome of the repeated refining of interpretations the researcher analyzed while engaging with the participants' own words.[30] In reaching interpretations it was important to preserve the soundness, consistency, and credibility of the interpretations by ensuring that the interpretations were connected to the participants' words in the transcript.[31]

84   *Appendix A: Methodology*

Reflexivity

It is important to note that IPA has a double hermeneutic nature.[32] As such, the researcher's interpretations of the participants' words are inseparable from the researcher's worldview and background. Additionally, in this study, the researcher herself is post-midlife and can be seen as not only researcher but also as participant. As the subject matter is close to the research analyst's heart, developmental life stage, and life experience, it was particularly important to exert caution and care during both data collection and data analysis in order to stay as true as possible to the participants' own voices and personal lived experiences. Whereas IPA acknowledges the researchers' unavoidable influence upon a study, it nonetheless requires the researcher to maintain a curious and open mind during the interview process, being careful to avoid predetermined conclusions. Additionally, during data analysis, the analyst used the transcript carefully as a means to engage with the participants' own words and experiences.

Ethical Concerns

Per the American Psychological Association's ethical standards the following basic principles were kept in mind:

Respect for Persons

Participants of this study were treated as free and autonomous. Each participant freely agreed in writing to participate in this study with no coercion or harmful consequences should they choose not to participate. Further, participants were free to end their participation in this study at any stage during its development. The investigator aimed to protect the welfare of the participants in the study including confidentiality in terms of their participation and the data collected from their participation. Further, clarifications about confidentiality were discussed prior to participants' engagement in the study and interviews. In order to uphold ethical standards of anonymity and privacy, detailed demographic data and identifying information was omitted in data analysis and results reported.

Beneficence

This study abided by the Hippocratic oath to "do no harm." In particular the researcher intended to minimize any harm such that participants were not willfully harmed physically, emotionally, or psychologically.

Justice

The researcher did not choose a population just because they were easily available, in a compromised position, or because they were open to manipulation. The sample was chosen based solely on the topic being studied and the criteria set forth in the Participants section above.

Types of Harm

Given the nature of psychological studies, it was difficult to ensure that absolutely no harm came to participants. This study asked for its participants to evaluate their lives and this was bound to arouse some difficult emotions. Nonetheless, the researcher tried to be sensitive to this possibility and provided referrals for counseling if the participant seemed vulnerable.

Coercion

The researcher explained the phenomenon to be explored in the study such that participants were not willfully misled to the nature of the study.

Notes

1 Biggerstaff & Thompson, 2008; Smith, 2004.
2 Henwood & Pidgeon, 1992; Smith, 1996a, 1996b, 2004; Turpin et al., 1997.
3 Barker, Pistrang, & Elliott, 2003; Creswell, 1998, 2014; Henwood & Pidgeon, 1992; Maxwell, 2005; Smith, 1996a, 1996b; Turpin et al., 1997.
4 Creswell, 2014.
5 Ibid.
6 Barker et al., 2003; Creswell, 2014; French, Maissi, & Marteau, 2005; Maxwell, 2005.
7 Biggerstaff & Thompson, 2008; Clare, 2003; French et al., 2005; Thompson, Kent, & Smith, 2002.
8 Biggerstaff & Thompson, 2008.
9 Ibid.
10 Ibid.
11 Smith, 2004.
12 Ibid.
13 Biggerstaff & Thompson, 2008; Smith, 2004.
14 Smith, 2004.
15 Ibid.
16 Smith, 2004, p. 44.
17 Smith, 2004.
18 Smith, 2004, p. 45.
19 Smith, 2004.
20 Ibid.

86   *Appendix A: Methodology*

21 Shinebourne & Smith, 2009.
22 Smith, Flowers, & Larkin, 2009.
23 Smith, 1996b; Smith & Osborn, 2007, p. 520.
24 Smith et al., 2009, p. 49.
25 Shinebourne & Smith, 2009; Smith et al., 2009.
26 Smith et al., 2009, p. 79.
27 Smith, 2004.
28 Smith et al., 2009, p. 79.
29 Shinebourne & Smith, 2009, p. 155.
30 Eatough & Smith, 2006.
31 Smith, Flowers & Larkin, 2009.
32 Ibid.

Appendix B
Screening and Interview Guides

Screening Guide

In order to determine whether a potential participant met the inclusion criteria the following questions were used as a guide:

1 Are you comfortable sharing your feelings regarding your life experiences?
2 How do you feel about reflecting upon the aging process?
3 Are there any factors that in your view would influence your ability to participate in this study, including any medical or psychological condition?

Interview Guide

The following questions were used as a guide in the 60–90 minute semistructured interview:

1 How do you make this time in your life meaningful?
2 What makes you feel satisfied and energized?
3 What makes you feel stuck and stagnant?
4 How have your values, priorities, and interests changed over time throughout your life and why?
5 How have your joys and fears changed over time throughout your life?
6 How do you experience the idea of life ending and facing death?

References

Adler, A. (1958). *What life should mean to you.* New York: Capricorn Books.

Administration on Aging. (2014). Aging statistics. *U.S. Department of Health and Human Services.* Retrieved from www.aoa.gov/Aging_Statistics/ [accessed October 19, 2015].

Angus, J. (2006). Ageism: A threat to "aging well" in the 21st century. *Journal of Applied Gerontology, 25*(2), 137–152. doi:10.1177/0733464805285745

Baltes, P. B., & Baltes, M. M. (1990). Psychological perspectives on successful aging: The model of selective optimization with compensation. In P. B. Baltes & M. M. Baltes (Eds.), *Successful aging: Perspectives from the behavioral sciences* (pp. 1–34). New York: Cambridge University Press.

Baltes, P. B., & Smith, J. (2003). New frontiers in the future of aging: From successful aging of the young old to the dilemmas of the fourth age. *Gerontology, 49*(2), 123–135. doi:10.1159/000067946

Barker, C., Pistrang, N., & Elliott, R. (2003). *Research methods in clinical psychology: An introduction for students and practitioners.* Hoboken, NJ: John Wiley.

Becker, G., Beyene, Y., Newsom, E., & Mayen, N. (2003). Creating continuity through mutual assistance: Intergenerational reciprocity in four ethnic groups. *The Journals of Gerontology. Series B, 58*(3), 151–159.

Bengtson, V., & Lowenstein, A. (2003). *Global aging and its challenge to families* (V. Bengtson & A. Lowenstein Eds.). New York: Aldine De Gruyter.

Biggerstaff, D., & Thompson, A. (2008). Interpretative phenomenological analysis (IPA): A qualitative methodology of choice in healthcare research. *Qualitative Research in Psychology, 5*(3), 214–224. doi:10.1080/14780880802314304

Blane, D., Wiggins, R., Montgomery, S., Hildon, Z., & Netuveli, G. (2011). Resilience at older ages: The importance of social relations and implications for policy. *International Centre for Life Course Studies in Society and Health* (3), 1–9.

Bloom, D., Canning, D., & Fink, G. (2010). Implications of population ageing for economic growth. *Oxford Review on Economic Policy*, 583–612. doi:10.1093/oxrep/grq038

Bookman, A. (2008). Innovative models of aging in place: Transforming our communities for an aging population. *Community, Work & Family, 11*(4), 419–438. doi:10.1080/13668800802362334

References 89

Börsch-Supan, A. (2003). Labor market effects of population aging. *Labour, 17,* 5–44. doi:10.1111/1467-9914.17.specialissue.2

Braam, A. W., Bramsen, I., van Tilburg, T. G., van der Ploeg, H. M., & Deeg, D. J. H. (2006). Cosmic transcendence and framework of meaning in life: Patterns among older adults in The Netherlands. *Journal of Gerontology: Social Sciences, 61B*(3), 121–128.

Brown, C., & Lowis, M. (2003). Psychosocial development in the elderly: An investigation into Erikson's ninth stage. *Journal of Aging Studies, 17*(4), 415–426. doi:10.1016/S0890-4065(03)00061-6

Calasanti, T. (2005). Ageism, gravity, and gender: Experiences of aging bodies. *Generations, 29*(3), 8–12.

Cambray, J. (2014). Emergence and longevity: Some psychological possibilities of later life. In L. Sawin, L. Corbett, & M. Carbine (Eds.), *Jung and aging: Possibilities and potentials for the second half of life* (pp. 43–59). New Orleans, LA: Spring Journal Books.

Caplan, L. (2011). The fear factor: Long-held predictions of economic chaos as baby boomers grow old are based on formulas that are just plain wrong. *The American Scholar, 3,* 18–29.

Carlson, M. C., Seeman, T., & Fried, L. P. (2000). Importance of generativity for healthy aging in older women. *Aging Clinical and Experimental Research, 12*(2), 132–140.

Carstensen, L., Turan, B., Scheibe, S., Ram, N., Ersner-Hershfield, H., Samanez-Larkin, G., ... Nesselroade, J. (2011). Emotional experience improves with age: Evidence based on over 10 years of experience sampling. *Psychology and Aging, 26*(1), 21–33.

Centers for Disease Control and Prevention. (2003). Public health and aging: Trends in aging—United States and worldwide. *The Journal of The American Medical Association, 289*(11). doi:10.1001

Clare, L. (2003). Managing threats to self: Awareness in early stage Alzheimer's disease. *Social Science & Medicine, 57*(6), 1017–1029.

Congressional Budget Office. (1999). *CBO memorandum: Projections of expenditures for long-term care services for the elderly.* Washington, DC.

Corbett, L. (2014a). A Jungian approach to spirituality in later life. In L. Sawin, L. Corbett, & M. Carbine (Eds.), *Jung and aging: Possibilities and potentials for the second half of life* (pp. 215–232). New Orleans, LA: Spring Journal Books.

Corbett, L. (2014b). Successful aging: Jungian contributions to development in later life. In L. Sawin, L. Corbett, & M. Carbine (Eds.), *Jung and aging: Possibilities and potentials for the second half of life* (pp. 19–39). New Orleans, LA: Spring Journal Books.

Costello, M. S. (2014). Conscious aging as a spiritual path. In L. Sawin, L. Corbett, & M. Carbine (Eds.), *Jung and aging: Possibilities and potentials for the second half of life* (pp. 151–175). New Orleans, LA: Spring Journal Books.

Coupland, J. (2007). Gendered discourses on the "problem" of ageing: Consumerized solutions. *Discourse & Communication, 1*(1), 37–61. doi:http://dx.doi.org/10.1177/1750481307071984

90   References

Creswell, J. W. (1998). *Qualitative enquiry and research design: Choosing among five traditions.* Thousand Oaks, CA: Sage.

Creswell, J. W. (2014). *Research design: Qualitative, quantitative, and mixed methods approaches.* Los Angeles, CA: Sage.

Crumbaugh, J. C., & Maholick, L. T. (1969). *Manual of instructions for the Purpose in Life Test.* Munster, IN: Psychometric Affiliates.

DaVanzo, J. (2001). Preparing for an aging world. *Rand Corporation.* Retrieved from www.rand.org/pubs/research_briefs/RB5058 [accessed October 19, 2015].

Eatough, V., & Smith, J. (2006). I was like a wild wild person: Understanding feelings of anger using interpretative phenomenological analysis. *British Journal of Psychology, 97*(4), 483–498.

Erikson, E. H. (1963). *Childhood and society.* New York: Norton.

Evans, J., & Niederehe, G. (2013). *A national institute of mental health perspective on geriatric mood disorder research.* New York: Oxford University Press.

Folts, W. E., & Muir, K. B. (2002). Housing for older adults: New lessons from the past. *Research On Aging, 24*(1), 10–28. doi:http://dx.doi.org/10.1177/01640275 03024001002

Frankenberg, E., & Thomas, D. (2011). Global aging. *Handbook of Aging and the Social Sciences* (7th ed., pp. 73–89). Elsevier.

Frankl, V. E. (1985). *Man's search for meaning.* New York: Pocket Books. (Original work published 1946.)

Frantz, G. (2014). *Sea glass: A Jungian exploration of suffering and individuation.* Cheyenne, WY: Fisher King Press.

Freedman, M. (2011). *The big shift: Navigating the new stage beyond midlife.* New York: Public Affairs.

Freedman, M. (2014). Encore: Mapping the route to second acts. In P. Irving & R. Beamish (Eds.), *The upside of aging: How long life is changing the worlds of health, work, innovation, policy and purpose.* Hoboken, NJ: Wiley.

Freeman, J. (1989). *Face to face.* London: British Broadcasting Corporation.

French, D. P., Maissi, E., & Marteau, T. M. (2005). The purpose of attributing cause: beliefs about the causes of myocardial infarction. *Social Science & Medicine, 60*(7), 1411–1421.

Futagami, K., & Nakajima, T. (2001). Population aging and economic growth. *Journal of Macroeconomics, 23*(1), 31–44. doi:10.1016/S0164-0704(01)00153-7

Garfein, A. J., & Herzog, A. R. (1995). Robust aging among the young-old, old-old, and oldest old. *The Journals of Gerontology, 50B*, S77–S87. doi:10.1093/geronb/50B.2.S77

Glass, T., Freedman, M., Carlson, M. C., Hill, J., Frick, K., Ialongo, N., ... Fried, L. P. (2004). Experience Corps: Design of an intergenerational program to boost social capital and promote the health of an aging society. *Journal of Urban Health, 81*(1), 94–105. doi:10.1093/jurban/jth096

Hanna, G. (2014). The central role of creativity in aging. In L. Sawin, L. Corbett, & M. Carbine (Eds.), *Jung and aging: Possibilities and potentials for the second half of life* (pp. 123–135). New Orleans, LA: Spring Journal Books.

Henwood, K., & Pidgeon, N. (1992). Qualitative research and psychological theorizing. *British Journal of Psychology, 83*, 97–111.

References 91

Hildon, Z., Montgomery, S., Blane, D., Wiggins, R., & Netuveli, G. (2010). Examining resilience of quality of life in the face of health-related and psychosocial adversity at older ages: What is "right" about the way we age? *The Gerontologist, 50*(1), 36–47. doi:10.1093/geront/gnp067

Hillman, J. (1999). *The force of character and the lasting life*. New York: Ballantine Books.

Hollis, J. (2005). *Finding meaning in the second half of life: How to finally really grow up*. New York: Gotham Books.

Hollis, J. (2014). For every tatter in our mortal dress: Stayin' alive at the front of the mortal parade. In L. Sawin, L. Corbett, & M. Carbine (Eds.), *Jung and aging: Possibilities and potentials for the second half of life* (pp. 201–214). New Orleans, LA: Spring Journal Books.

Irving, P. H. (2014). *The upside of aging: How long life is changing the world of health, work, innovation, policy and purpose*. Hoboken, NJ: John Wiley & Sons.

James, W. (1902). *The varieties of religious experience: A study of human nature*. London, UK: Longmans, Green.

Johnson, R., & Ruhl, J. (2007). *Living your unlived life: Coping with unrealized dreams and fulfilling your purpose in the second half of life*. New York: Tarcher/Penguin.

Jorm, A. F., Christensen, H., Henderson, A. S., Jacomb, P. A., Korten, A. E., & Mackinnon, A. (1998). Factors associated with successful aging. *Australasian Journal on Ageing, 17*, 33–37.

Ju, H., Shin, J. W., Kim, C. W., Hyun, M. H., & Park, J. W. (2013). Mediational effect of meaning in life on the relationship between optimism and well-being in community elderly. *Archives of Gerontology and Geriatrics, 56*(2), 308–313. doi:10.1016/j.archger.2012.08.008.

Jung, C. G. (1960). The stages of life. (R. F. C. Hull, Trans.) In G. Adler & R. F. C. Hull (Series Eds.), *The collected works of C.G. Jung* (Vol. 8). Princeton, NJ: Princeton University Press. (Original work published 1930.)

Jung, C. G. (1971). *Modern man in search of a soul*. San Diego, CA: Harcourt Brace Jovanovich. (Original work published 1933.)

Jung, C. G. (1989). *Memories, dreams, reflections*. New York: Vintage. (Original work published 1961.)

Kinsella, K., & Phillips, D. (2005). Global aging: The challenge of success. *Population Bulletin, 60*(1), 1–44.

Knickman, J., & Snell, E. (2002). The 2030 problem: Caring for aging baby boomers. *Health Services Research, 37*(4), 849–884. doi:http://dx.doi.org/10.1034/j.1600-0560.2002.56.x

Kochera, A., Straight, A., & Guterbock, T. (2005). Beyond 50.05: A report to the nation on livable communities—Creating environments for successful aging. *AARP*, 1–112.

Krause, N. (2012). Meaning in life and healthy aging. In P. Wong (Ed.), *The human quest for meaning* (pp. 409–432). New York: Routledge.

Kulik, C., Ryan, S., Harper, S., & George, G. (2014). Aging populations and management. *Academy of Management, 57*(4), 929–935. doi:10.5465/amj.2014.4004

92   References

Laslett, P. (1989). *A fresh map of life: The emergence of the third age.* London: Weidenfeld and Nicolson.

Lavretsky, H., Sajatovic, M., & Reynolds III, C. (2013). Preface. In H. Lavretsky, M. Sajatovic, & C. Reynolds III (Eds.), *Late-life mood disorders* (pp. xix–xx). New York: Oxford University Press.

Lawrence-Lightfoot, S. (2009). *The third chapter: Passion, risk and adventure in the 25 years after 50.* New York: Sarah Crichton Books.

Levy, B., Chung, P., Bedford, T., & Navrazhina, K. (2014). Faceboook as a site for negative age stereotypes. *The Gerontologist, 54*(2), 172–176.

Library of Congress. (2012). News from the Library of Congress. Retrieved from www.loc.gov/today/pr/2012/12-026.html [accessed October 11, 2015].

Lloyd-Sherlock, P. (2000). Population ageing in developed and developing regions: Implications for health policy. *Social Science & Medicine (2000), 51*(6), 887–895. doi:http://dx.doi.org/10.1016/S0277-9536(00)00068-X

Malette, J., & Oliver, L. (2006). Retirement and existential meaning in the older adult: A qualitative study using life review. *Counselling, Psychotherapy, and Health, 2*(1), 30–49.

Malinen, S., & Johnston, L. (2013). Workplace ageism: Discovering hidden bias. *Experimental Aging Research, 39*, 445–465. doi:10.1080/0361073X.2013.808111

Martens, A., Goldenberg, J. L., & Greenberg, J. (2005). A terror management perspective on ageism. *Journal of Social Issues, 61*, 223–229.

Martens, A., & Peedicayil, J. (2012). A comparison of Erikson's Epigenetic Principle with epigenetics. *Journal of Theoretical Biology, 315*, 144–145. doi:10.1016/j.jtbi.2012.09.010

Maslow, A. (1962). *Toward a psychology of being.* New York: Van Nostrand.

Matthews, J., & Turnbull, G. (2008). Housing the aging baby boomers: Implications for local policy. *Andrew Young School of Policy Studies Research Paper Series*, 1–32.

Mattoon, M. A. (2005). *Jung and the human psyche.* New York: Routledge.

Maxwell, J. A. (2005). *Qualitative research design: An interactive approach* (2nd ed.). Thousand Oaks, CA: Sage.

Mermin, G., Johnson, R., & Toder, E. (2008). Will employers want aging boomers? *Urban Institute.* Retrieved from www.urban.org/url.cfm?ID=411705 [accessed October 21, 2015].

Morgan, K., Dallosso, H., Bassey, E. J., Ebrahim, S., Fentem, P. H., & Arie, T. H. D. (1991). Customary physical activity, psychological well-being and successful aging. *Ageing and Society, 11*, 399–415.

Morgan, R. (2014). What the future of aging means to all of us: An era of possibilities. *Indiana Law Review, 48*, 125–148.

Nakagawa, T. (2007). Exploratory research on gerotranscendence of the Japanese elderly living in the community. *Japanese Journal of Gerontology, 29*(2), 202.

Netburn, D. (August 24, 2016). The aging paradox: The older we get, the happier we are. *Los Angeles Times.* Retrieved from www.latimes.com/science/science now/la-sci-sn-older-people-happier-20160824-snap-story.html [accessed September 1, 2016].

References 93

O'Donohue, J. (1997). *Anam Cara: A book of Celtic wisdom.* New York: Harper Perennial.

Perry, V., & Wolburg, J. (2011). Aging gracefully: Emerging issues for public policy and consumer welfare. *Journal of Consumer Affairs, 45*(3), 365–371. doi:http://dx.doi.org/10.1111/j.1745-6606.2011.01208.x

Reker, G. (2001). Prospective predictors of successful aging in community-residing and institutionalized Canadian elderly. *Ageing International, 27*(1), 42–64. doi:10.1007/s12126-001-1015-4

Rogers, C. R. (1980). *A way of being.* New York: Houghton Mifflin.

Rowe, J. W., & Kahn, R. L. (1997). Successful aging. *The Gerontologist, 37*, 433–440.

Ruhl, J., & Evans, R. (2014). Spirituality and relationship in later life. In L. Sawin, L. Corbett, & M. Carbine (Eds.), *Jung and aging: Possibilities and potentials for the second half of life* (pp. 179–199). New Orleans, LA: Spring Journal Books.

Ryff, C. D. (1989). Beyond Ponce de Leon and life satisfaction: New directions in quest of successful aging. *International Journal of Behavioral Development, 12*, 35–55.

Sawin, L. (2014). The case for a Jungian view of aging. In L. Sawin, L. Corbett, & M. Carbine (Eds.), *Jung and aging: Possibilities and potentials for the second half of life.* New Orleans, LA: Spring Journal Books.

Scarcello, J. (2010). *Fifty and fabulous: The best years of a woman's life.* London, UK: Duncan Baird.

Schoklitsch, A., & Baumann, U. (2012). Generativity and aging: A promising future research topic? *Journal of Aging Studies, 26*, 262–272. doi:10.1016/j.jaging.2012.01.002

Schulz, R., & Heckhausen, J. (1996). A life span model of successful aging. *American Psychologist, 51*, 702–714.

Shinebourne, P., & Smith, J. A. (2009). Alcohol and self: An interpretive phenomenological analysis of the experience of addictions and its impact on the sense of self and identity. *Addiction Research and Theory, 17* (2), 152–167.

Sinnott, J. (2009). Complex thought and construction of the self in the face of aging and death. *Journal of Adult Development, 16*(3), 155–165. doi:10.1007/s10804-009-9057-z

Smith, J. (1996a). Beyond the divide between cognition and discourse: Using interpretative phenomenological analysis in health psychology. *Psychology & Health, 11*(2), 261–271. doi:10.1080/08870449608400256

Smith, J. (1996b). Qualitative methodology: Analyzing participants' perspectives. *Current Opinion in Psychiatry, 9*, 417–421.

Smith, J. (2004). Reflecting on the development of interpretative phenomenological analysis and its contribution to qualitative research in psychology. *Qualitative Research in Psychology, 1*(1), 39–54. doi:10.1191/1478088704qp004oa

Smith, J., Flowers, P., & Larkin, M. (2009). *Interpretative phenomenological analysis: Theory, method and research.* Los Angeles, CA: Sage.

Smith, J., & Osborn, M. (2007). Pain as an assault on the self: An interpretative phenomenological analysis of the psychological impact of chronic benign low back pain. *Psychology and Health, 22*(5), 517–534.

94 References

Smith, S. K., Rayer, S., Smith, E., Wang, Z., & Zeng, Y. (2012). Population aging, disability and housing accessibility: Implications for sub-national areas in the United States. *Housing Studies, 27*(2), 252–266. doi:10.1080/02673037. 2012.649468

Steger, M. F., Frazier, P., Oishi, S., & Kaler, M. (2006). The Meaning in Life Questionnaire: Assessing the presence of and search for meaning in life. *Journal of Counseling Psychology, 53*, 30–93.

Swift, H. J., Abrams, D., Lamont, R. A., & Drury, L. (2017). The risks of ageism model: How ageism and negative attitudes toward age can be a barrier to active aging. *Social Issues and Policy Review, 11*, 195–231. doi:10.1111/sipr.12031

Tennyson, A. (1860). "Tithonus." Retrieved from www.poetryfoundation.org/poem/174656 [accessed October 23, 2015].

Thomas, M., Kaufmann, C., Palmer, B., Depp, C., Martin, A., Glorioso, D., ... & Jeste, D. (2016). Paradoxical trend for improvement in mental health with aging: A community-based study of 1,546 adults aged 21–100 years. *The Journal of Clinical Psychiatry, 77*(8), e1019–e1025. doi:10.4088/JCP.16m10671

Thompson, A., Kent, G., & Smith, J. (2002). Living with vitiligo: Dealing with difference. *British Journal of Health Psychology, 7*(2), 213–225. doi:10.1348/135910702169457

Tornstam, L. (1997). Gerotranscendence: The contemplative dimensions of aging. *Journal of Aging Studies, 11*, 143–154.

Tornstam, L. (2005). *Gerotranscendence: A developmental theory of positive aging.* New York: Springer.

Tornstam, L. (2011). Maturing into gerotranscendence. *The Journal of Transpersonal Psychology, 43*(2), 166–180.

Tosun, M. (2003). Population aging and economic growth: Political economy and open economy effects. *Economics Letters, 81*(3), 291–296. doi:10.1016/S0165-1765(03)00195-2

Turpin, G., Barley, V., Beail, N., Scaife, J., Slade, P., Smith, J., & Walsh, S. (1997). Standards for research projects and theses involving qualitative methods: Suggested guidelines for trainees and courses. *Clinical Psychology Forum, 108*, 3–7.

United Nations, Department of Economic and Social Affairs, Population Division (2013). *World Population Ageing 2013.* ST/ESA/SER.A/348. Retrieved from www.un.org [accessed October 19, 2015].

van der Gaag, J., & Precker, A. (1997). *Health care for an aging population: Issues and options.* Washington, DC: World Bank.

Villar, F. (2012). Successful ageing and development: The contribution of generativity in older age. *Ageing and Society, 32*(7), 1087–1105. doi:10.1017/S0144686X11000973

von Humboldt, S., Leal, I., & Pimenta, F. (2014). Does spirituality really matter? A study on the potential of spirituality for older adult's adjustment to aging. *The Japanese Psychological Association, 56*(2), 114–125.

Warburton, J., McLaughlin, D., & Pinsker, D. (2006). Generative acts: family and community involvement of older Australians. *International Journal of Aging & Human Development, 63*(2), 115–137. doi:10.2190/9TE3-T1G1-333V-3DT8

References 95

Winsor, M. (2015). China's one-child policy may be replaced with "two-child" law, after 35 Years. *International Business Times*. Retrieved from www.ibtimes.com/chinas-one-child-policy-change-will-take-decades-relieve-economic-pressures-aging-2161789 [accessed November 6, 2015].

Xu, J., Kochanek, K. D., Murphy, S. L., & Arias, E. (2014). *Mortality in the United States, 2012. NCHS Data Brief.* Retrieved from www.cdc.gov [accessed October 19, 2015].

Yeh, C. (2015). Fostering a new world view on aging. *Journal of the American Society, 39*(1), 10–15.

Zanjiran, S., Keyani, L., Zare, M., & Shayeghian, Z. (2015). The effectiveness of group logotherapy on the sense of loneliness of elderly women resident in nursing homes. *Knowledge and Research in Applied Psychology 16*(3), 60–67.

Zeiger, G. (2000). Old soul: How aging reveals character – A conversation with James Hillman. *The Sun Magazine*.

Index

AARP 20; *see also* American Association of Retired Persons
ability 22, 24, 54, 56, 58–9, 65–6, 69, 71, 78, 80; athletic 21; changing 16; cognitive 75; explanatory 73; society's 66
access to relationships 70
accountants 50
activities 5, 7–8, 15–16, 32–4, 37, 40–1, 43–5, 47, 50, 64; creative 43; daily 37; life-affirming 41, 64
adaptation 19, 25–6, 35; aversive 25, 52; optimal 15
adjustment 18, 20, 25, 35
administrators 39
adolescence 71
adult children 22, 31, 39, 50, 82
adult consumers 9
adulthood 22–3, 33, 35–6, 38–40, 43–4, 51–2, 54–5, 57–60, 63, 77; early 1, 25, 35, 52; older 44, 64, 77–8; younger 20–1
adults 3, 7, 9, 22, 27, 48, 53, 63, 70; post-midlife 63; working age 3; young 38, 60
Advanced Leadership Initiative, The (Harvard) 72
adventure 69, 77
adversity 56, 61–2
advertising 9
aerial stunt performers 73
affirmation of life 31, 33–48, 64
affluent neighborhoods 9
age 1–2, 7, 9, 14–28, 31, 34–5, 64, 66, 68–70, 74–7; chronological 79; earlier 21; integration 7; older 16,

61, 70, 76; working 4; younger 15, 36
ageism 4, 10; combatting 10; personal 68
ageist attitudes 9
aging 1–2, 4–8, 10, 14–15, 17–20, 22–4, 27, 63, 71, 73–6; adults 18, 40; conscious 23; and death 10; demographic 2, 4; experience 82; investigated 14; likened 27; paradox 74; parents 72; physical 9, 20; population 4–5, 7, 11; positive experience of 17; process 1, 14, 16, 18, 20, 27–8, 31, 43, 76, 81
aging-in-place organizations 7, 9
American Association of Retired Persons (AARP) Foundation 20
American culture 5
American Psychological Association 84
Americans 3, 72
Angus, J. 10–11
anxiety 33, 74
anxiousness 78
approaches 14, 31, 71, 77, 79, 82; educational 71; idiographic 82; integrated 14; multidimensional 14
artistic pursuits 44
artists 78; folk 24; professional 24; untrained 24
asexual behavior 10
Asia 3
aspirations 28, 68
assertiveness 21
AtA 20; *see also* adjustment to aging

Index 97

attributes 76, 79; negative 74; protective 61; of qualitative research 79

baby boom children 5
bacterial infections 45, 51
Baltes, M.M. 14–15
Baltes, P.B. 14–15
Baltes model 15
barriers 19, 68; down 10; new 10; old 20
battle wounds 76
Bedford, T. 10
befriending people 52
behavioral changes 74
beliefs 76
beneficence 84
big data and in-depth data 73
biological pressures 16
biological properties 14
biology 18, 76
birth 3, 16, 21, 49
bodies 26, 41, 69, 73; and minds 9, 43; scholarly 14
book groups 43
borders 19, 69–70; new 70; traditional 69–70
boundaries 70; crossing disciplinary 70; crossing gender 70; crossing generational 70; crossing geographic 70
breast cancer 57, 66
British psychology 79
businesses 8, 38, 56, 69

campus 8, 69; affiliated communities 9; affiliated residences 7–8
cancer 36, 57; colon 35; pancreatic 36
capacity 35, 44; building 41, 53; individual's 15; physical functional 14; society's 24
care 3, 5–7, 17, 34, 84; elder 9; formal 6; and housing for older adults 7; medical 8; preventative 6
careers 25, 33, 35, 44, 49, 52, 58, 67, 72, 76
caregivers 6, 22, 27, 68; volunteer 6
caretakers 51
caring society 8, 35
Carstensen, Laura 75

Centers for Disease Control and Prevention 2
childhood 49, 54, 58
children 3, 26, 38–9, 41–2, 46, 48–9, 52, 58, 60, 67; isolated 27; school-age 66; young 3
China 3
chronic activation 75
chronic constipation 59
chronic coughing 59
Chung, P. 10
classes 57, 61, 69–70
clinical studies 16
clinicians 63–5
coffee table conversations 73
cognition 74
cognitive processes 31, 43, 80
college education 42
college students 67
colonoscopies 35
community 5–10, 15, 17, 34, 48, 53, 61, 64, 72, 76; care 6; colleges 72; design 7; expectations 35; experiences 53; faith 23; human 25; important 6; involvement 17; organizations 42; relationships 53; roles 22; work 38
computers 61, 69, 76
confidentiality 33, 84
Congressional Budget Office (CBO) 5
connections 24, 32, 46, 48, 50, 52, 54, 58, 64; interpersonal 66, 68, 70; losing 83; past childhood 48; strong 37, 80; transpersonal 28
Corbett, Lionel 21, 24, 40, 43–4, 50, 52, 54
Costello, M.S. 23, 25, 36
Coupland, J. 9
coursework 67, 69
creative life 79
creative processes 44
creativity 10, 20, 24, 32, 41, 43–4
crisis 16, 18, 40
cultural messages 68, 70
culture 68, 70
curiosity 26, 43, 46

data analysis 31, 79, 83–4
data collection 82, 84

98 *Index*

death 10, 18–20, 24–5, 27, 35–7, 52, 57, 64, 75, 77; early 37; idea of 35, 75; inevitability of 27; mother's 57; release 25; viewed 35
debilitation 9
demographers 2–3
dependency ratios 3
depth psychologists 75–7; *see also* psychologists
depth psychology 73, 75, 77–8
development 4, 14, 16–17, 21, 26, 28, 62, 68, 70, 84
developmental milestones 63
developmental stages 16, 40; of generativity 40; new 63
developmental tasks 20–1, 24, 40, 64
disabilities 10, 15, 76; disease-related 14; lower 5
disciplines 14
discrimination 4
disease 10, 14
Disease Control 2
doctoral studies 67, 69
double hermeneutic 80
dreams 27, 67–8, 71
dynamic balance 28

economic burdens 5–6
economy 2–3, 11
education 3, 6, 34, 71–2
educators 33–4, 45, 50
elder care and housing 9
elderly people 10
elders 5–8, 22, 50, 64; contribution 10; keeping 8
emotional times 33
energy 21–2, 24, 26, 46, 57, 70
energy level 57
engagement 8, 19, 24, 40, 44, 46–7, 76, 84; personal 23; researcher's 80; social 61, 65
enthusiasm 26, 41, 46, 61
environments 14, 23, 50; cultural 16; dynamic 67; supportive 23, 50
epigenesis 16
Erikson, Erik 16, 40, 54; developmental model 16; developmental stage of generativity vs. stagnation 17, 53; theory of generativity 17; theory personality 16

Erikson, Joan 16
Europe 3
Evans, J. 23–4, 50, 54
excitement 41–3, 69
existence 17–18, 38, 62, 66, 74; and finding ultimate meaning during one's 55; human 15, 66, 77–8
experience 17, 19, 21–2, 28, 38, 40, 49, 59, 69–70, 72; emotional 54; exhilarating 69; and fulfillment in life 56; inner 31; participant's 83; personal 27, 54, 69, 80; positive 17; relationships 69

family 1, 3, 5, 21–2, 34–5, 48, 50, 54–5, 64, 67; beautiful 55; building 76; business 34, 38; caregivers 6; commitments 24; configuration 52; extended 48, 58; and friends 5, 22, 64; frustrations 58; highlighted 50; human 64; members 24; roles 22; systems 3; units 3
fear 10, 26, 34–7, 46; of death 37; harbored 75
Frankl, Viktor 16–18, 40, 61–2
Frantz, Gilda 27, 36, 43
Freedman, Marc 17, 71–2
freedom 33, 72
Freeman, J. 77
Fried, Linda 17
friends 5–6, 32, 34, 37, 48, 50–5, 58, 60, 64, 67; and family caregivers 6; male 34; old 24; and retired doctors 60
friendships 22, 38, 52; long-time 52; new 22, 24, 65
functional imaging studies 74
funds of knowledge 22, 40

gap year 71–2
gardening work 61
general economy 3–4
generations 2, 4, 10, 16–17, 38–40, 54; earlier 19; new 16
generativity 16–17, 40, 53, 70; changes 16; in older adults 16–17; in relation to samples of older Australians 17
gerontologists 2, 9
gerontology fields 14
gifts 1, 46, 55, 64, 67, 69, 71, 76–8

Index 99

girlfriends 51; close 36; cultivated 52; new 51
Glass, T. 17
glazing 37, 44
global aging 3
goals, life-long 21
God 36, 38, 51, 53
grandchildren 22, 38–9, 43, 48–50, 58, 60–1
grandmothers 44, 49
grandparents 22, 31, 48, 50, 55, 82
groups 10, 24, 31, 37, 69, 79; book club 43; Facebook 9, 69; women's 34
growth 6, 25, 28, 45–7, 52, 62, 68, 70–2; internal 19, 76; new 71; personal 14, 46, 68; spiritual 20, 23, 50, 76

Hanna, G. 24, 44
happiness 72, 75
health 8, 11, 20, 23, 57, 59; better 15; deteriorates 61; emotional 7; excellent 15, 76; good 56; inequalities 6; levels 17; services 4, 6
health care providers 8
healthcare 4–5
healthcare systems 3–4, 11
healthy aging 5–6
hiking 45
Hillman, James 75–6
histories 52, 55, 57
Hollis, James 25–6, 35, 43, 46, 52
home care 5, 8
homes 7–9, 39, 57, 60, 67
hospital administrators 50
hours 8, 42–4, 61; of study 8; of work 61
housing 3, 7–9
human connections 48, 54, 64, 68
human developmental process 20, 22, 66
human relationships 48, 52–4, 64; and finding a meaning in later life 48; and resiliency 48–62
human spirit 17, 62, 65
humanities 77–8
husbands 16, 35, 45, 48–9, 51, 59–60, 67, 75

illnesses 17, 24, 51, 56, 62

images 9, 23–4, 34, 81
imaging studies 74
individuals 1–3, 9–10, 19, 21, 23–6, 31, 33, 52, 79, 81–2; autistic 41; enabled 66; encouraged 25; helping 18, 53; older 4, 74
individuals post-midlife 2
individuation process (Jung) 16, 19, 21, 28, 35, 52
insecurities 58, 68
interests 1, 10, 21–2, 26, 39, 41, 44, 46, 50, 61; new 50; pursued 41; shared 50
intergenerational reciprocity functions 3
interpersonal connection and relationships 66, 68, 70
interpretations 80–1, 83; phenomenological analysis 31, 73; researcher's 84
interpreters 80–1
Interpretive Phenomenological Analysis 31, 75, 79–82, 84
interviews 1, 19, 28, 31, 33, 38, 80–4; focus group 17; qualitative 19; semi-structured 82–3
IPA 31, 75, 79–82, 84; *see also* Interpretive Phenomenological Analysis
IPA methodology 31, 81
IPA stages 83

Johnson, R. 27
Jung, Carl 16, 19–23, 24, 28, 35, 43, 44, 67, 75–7; symposium, *Jung and Aging: Bringing to Life the Possibilities and Potentials for Vital Aging* 20
Jungian elder 27
Jungian perspective 36
Jungian psychology 28
Jungian tradition 25

kids 39, 58
Knickman, J. 3, 5
knowledge 14, 17, 22, 40, 46, 60–1, 76–8; advanced 16; base 15; to teach 61; of tools 76; and wisdom 40
Kulik, C. 3

100 *Index*

Lawrence-Lightfoot, Sarah 70
lawyers 50
learning 20, 32, 34, 41–6, 51, 53, 61,
  69–71; attitudes 47; endeavors 43;
  new 70
legacy 16, 38, 40
lessons 25, 43, 46
levels 7, 55–6, 66–7, 69, 80–1; higher
  educational 15, 18, 74; macro 53;
  micro 53; multiple 66; psychological
  80
life 1–2, 6, 9, 14–17, 19–28, 31–50,
  52–69, 71, 73–4, 76–8, 87–94;
  activities 37; circumstances 56,
  58–60, 62, 82; experience 22, 66,
  68–9, 71, 84; history 18
life-long learning 45–6, 64
life-long participants 24, 44
Life Review 18, 55, 65
life stages 26, 33, 70, 72;
  developmental 1, 84; new 71–2
lifespan 16, 35, 44–5, 64, 66–8; defined
  40; demographics 2, 11; human 20;
  increasing 31
literature 36, 40, 43–4, 46, 50, 53–5,
  61–2, 71; and myth 25; reviews 82
logotherapy 17, 18, 62, 65
long-term care 5–6
long-term relationships 23
Los Angeles Times 74
losses 1, 9–10, 14–15, 18, 20, 24–5, 58,
  64, 67, 74; early 58; multiple 23;
  possible 64
love 43, 45, 49, 56–7, 61, 78;
  experiences 49; learning 43;
  literature 43; relationships 23;
  science 61
LR 18, 55, 65; *see also* Life Review

Malette, J. 18
marriages 52
Martens, A. 10, 18
maturity 16, 22, 33, 40
McLaughlin, D. 17
Meaning Life Questionnaire 17
media 9
Medicaid 5
medical resilience 56
mental health 2, 66, 74
middle age 27–8, 63, 70–1

midlife 16; and generativity 16; and old
  age 2, 71–2
MLQ 17; *see also* Meaning Life
  Questionnaire
models 7–8, 14, 16, 63, 71, 80; medical
  14; new 6–7, 9; third aging-in-place
  8; traditional one-on-one 6; "village"
  8
Morgan, K. 15
mortality 10, 35, 37, 40, 57
mothers 35–9, 49, 57–9, 67
mothers-in-law 58
motivators 35, 75

Navrazhina, K. 10
negative life events 61, 65
New Outlook 1–11, 14
NORCs 7–8; *see also* naturally
  occurring retirement communities
North America 3
nursing homes 5–6, 18
nurturing 34, 54

O'Donohue, John 73, 78
old age 2, 18–19, 27, 40, 63, 70–2, 76;
  viewed 19; wisdom 76
older adults 1–4, 6–7, 9–11, 17–20,
  22–4, 26–8, 44, 63–5, 68–72, 74–7
older population 3–4, 17
older women 18, 52

pain 9, 45, 56, 67, 80–1
parents 26, 35, 39, 58, 67–8
participants 24, 27–8, 33–8, 40–1,
  43–5, 48, 50–1, 57, 74–5, 80–5;
  active 8; post-midlife 39; potential
  82; returning 24, 44
passion 1, 42–3, 53, 61, 69; great 43;
  personal 26
personal development 19, 76
personal goal attainment 14
personal relationships 19, 27, 38
personality types 16, 21, 52, 70, 75
persons 2, 19, 21, 23–4, 27–8, 34, 36,
  42–4, 53, 55; insecure 57; single 45
perspectives 10, 18, 20, 39, 46, 70,
  75–6, 82; maintaining of 20;
  personal 31, 79, 81; public policy 71;
  unique 28
physical deterioration 57

Index 101

physical health 74–5; *see also* health
Pinsker, D. 17
poetry 73, 78
population 2–3, 63, 82, 85; levels 74;
  older adult 3
population aging 4–5, 7, 11
post-midlife 1–2, 40, 43, 46, 58, 83–4;
  adults 63; meaning-making 39, 46,
  81
pottery 34, 37, 43–4, 54
predictors for successful aging 15
professional volunteers 6, 17, 34, 36
psych hospitals 58
psychological approaches 77
psychological battles 81
psychological beings 17, 62
psychological benefits 23
psychological functions 21
psychological obstacles 46
psychological problems 56, 62
psychological resilience 57–8
psychological studies 85
psychology 67, 79; fields 14;
  qualitative 80; scholarship 15;
  unconscious feminine 21;
  unconscious masculine 21
Purpose in Life Test (PIL) 17

qualitative research 75, 79; methods 31;
  software 83; studies 17
qualitative studies 18, 28, 73, 75, 77
quality relationships 61
quantitative research methodologies
  79

randomized controlled trials 79
RCT 79; *see also* randomized
  controlled trials
referrals 82, 85
Reker, G. 15
relationships 20, 22–3, 32, 38–9, 49,
  51–4, 58, 68–70, 83; access to 70;
  adversarial 71; communal 53;
  difficult 59; direct 53;
  intergenerational 69, 71; intimate 23,
  67; multiple 39; parent-child 39;
  strong 50
research 4, 6, 8, 14, 16–17, 19–20, 23,
  33, 41, 79; analysts 80; approach 79;
  dissertations 69; human 80; on-line

61; phenomenological 80;
  quantitative 31, 79; studies 82
researchers 31, 45, 79–85
resiliency 22–3, 32, 48–62, 65; best 60;
  to life's circumstances 60; in older
  age 61; psychological 58
responsibilities 9, 22–3, 40, 59, 63–4, 77
retirement 2, 18, 24, 53
role models 24, 68
Rosemary B. Fuss Center for Research
  on Aging and Intergenerational
  Studies 8
Ruhl, J. 23–4, 27, 43, 50, 54

Sawin, L. 19
Scarcello, J. 20
school administrators 59
school districts 41
schools 8, 17, 21, 39, 42, 56, 69, 80;
  high 44, 54; underserved elementary
  17
science 43, 49–50, 61, 70;
  philosophical 79; teachers 43;
  teaching of 60; true 77
self 16, 18–19, 23, 25–8, 32, 47, 52, 55,
  64, 68; acceptance 14, 27;
  actualization 34; authentic 25, 35,
  52; autonomous 81; ever-emerging
  23; old 81; personal 27; strong 81;
  vulnerable 81; young 1
self-ageism 67
self-awareness 34
self-confidence 27
self-esteem 9, 21–2, 24, 40, 44
self-reflection 33, 46
self-trust 73
self-understanding 33, 35, 40
services 5–8, 41, 71
Smith, Jonathan 79–81, 83
Snell, E. 3, 5
social determinants 11
social media 10, 69
social perspectives 2, 11
social phenomena 31, 79
social policy analysts 2, 4–5
social relationships 19, 21
societal obligations 34
society 1–4, 6–7, 9–11, 20, 22, 25, 64,
  66, 70–2, 76–7; attitudes of 11;
  contemporary 3; modern 9, 64

102 *Index*

soul 14, 25–6, 34–5, 41, 64, 69, 73, 76–8; elevated 76; of humankind 77; and individual character 76; searching 26, 40, 46

spirituality 20, 22, 26, 28, 37, 40; deepening 19; development of 23; infused 37; mature 26; popularizing Celtic 73

spouses 24, 51–2, 58

school counselors 51

stagnation 16–17, 40, 53

stereotypes 10–11, 68; internalized 68; negative age 9–10

students 8, 38, 46, 69; and elders 8; full-time 8

study 4, 17–21, 33–6, 43–4, 52, 54–7, 62–3, 73–5, 79–82, 84–5; of astronomy 46; of geology 46; and interviews 84; of social phenomena and psychology 79

"successful aging" (Hillman) 14–15, 24, 61, 76

support 3, 6–7, 42, 67, 72, 74; income 3; for older people 3; research designs 75

supportive activities 16, 40

supportive services 3, 7

symposium, *Jung and Aging: Bringing to Life the Possibilities and Potentials for Vital Aging* 20

teachers 38, 46

technology and knowledge 60

Tennyson, Alfred Lord 25

test scales: Meaning Life Questionnaire (MLQ) 17; Purpose in Life Test (PIL) 17

themes 18, 31, 33, 39–40, 46, 48, 83; emerging 83; recurring 40; significant 48; superordinate 83; table of 83

Tithonus 25

Tornstam, L. 19–20

United Jewish Communities 7

United States 3, 7

universities 8, 74

values 5, 19, 28, 40, 42, 52–3, 76; core 28; significant economic 6

villagers 7–8

villages and campus-affiliated communities 9

Villar, F. 16, 40

volunteers 6, 17, 34, 36

von Humboldt, S. 20

Warburton, J. 17

wisdom 17–18, 20, 22, 28, 32, 39–40, 68–70, 72, 74, 78; imparting of 39; and knowledge 17; sharing 39–40

women 1, 15, 20–1, 31, 35, 37, 40–1, 51–2, 56–7, 73–4; and descriptions of life 73; featured 75; and friends 51; married 82; post-midlife 1, 28, 36; voices of 28, 31, 48, 63

work 4, 19, 21–3, 41, 43, 45, 56, 58–61, 70–2, 80; clinical 64, 67; doctoral 67; environment 4; existential 65; part-time 41, 44; and society 7; volunteer 41

workforce 4, 6

working age people 3–4

workplace discrimination charges 4

yoga 45

younger adults 74

younger workers 3

Zanjiran, S. 18

PGMO 04/25/2018